Mesozoic Fossils II
The Cretaceous Period

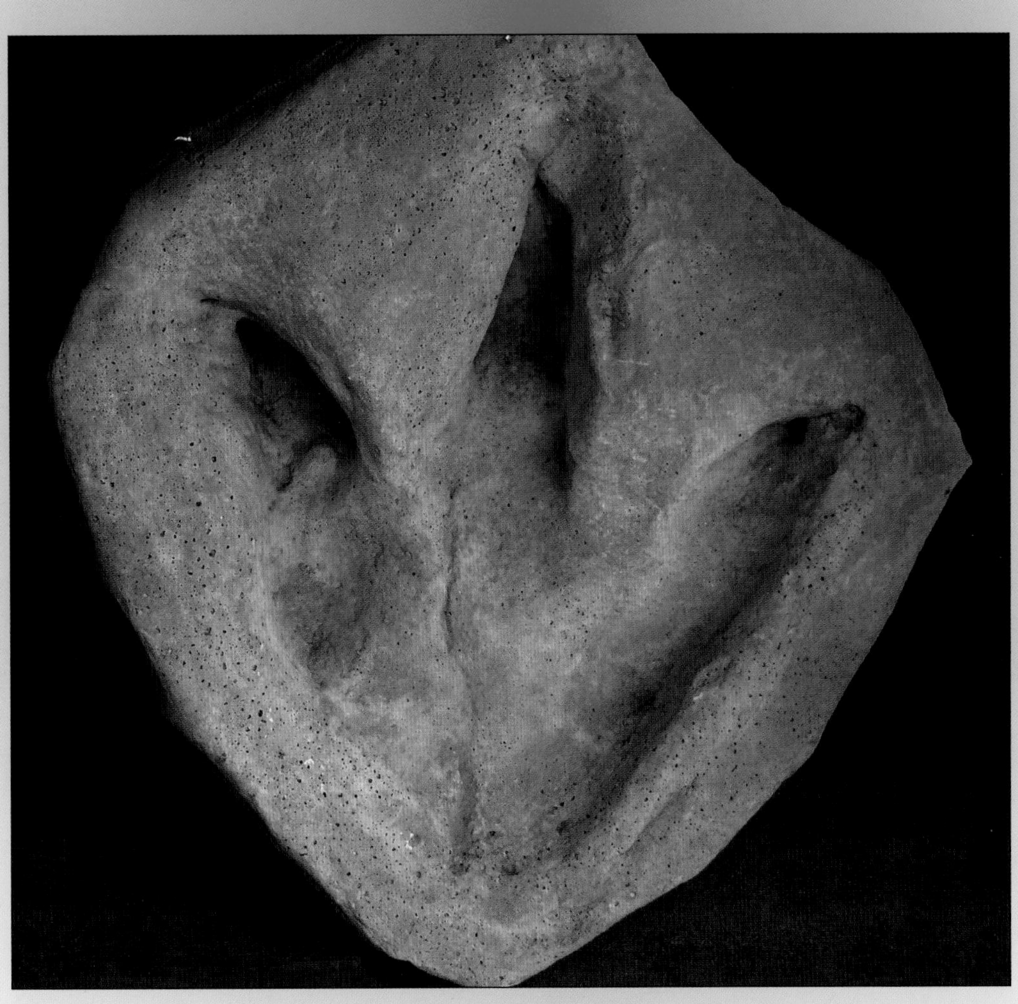

Bruce L. Stinchcomb

4880 Lower Valley Road, Atglen, Pennsylvania 19310

The Value of Cretaceous Fossils and Value Guide

The uninformed, seeing monetary values placed upon fossils (which if you put in the right kind of effort you can find yourself), are sometimes attracted to them as a perceived source of easy money. Nothing could be further from the truth. Yes, one can often find fossils, but it's not like finding money. What has to be considered is the completeness, rarity, and appearance of the fossil. Fossils can be common, some whole layers of rock are entirely composed of them but these generally have no commercial value. What also has to be considered is the effort and time invested in their preparation, the removal of excess rock and the exposure of the fossil. With many fossils, including many Mesozoic fossils such as ammonites, such "value added" labor in polishing has to be considered in a fossil's value and price. Most fossils don't look like much in the field; they have to be brought out (prepared) from the rock by painstaking manual methods or by technology, using such devices such as pneumatic chisels, air abrasive machines, acids or other chemicals. Fossil preparation strategies are varied and the list is extensive, as fossil preparation is a field in itself. It should be pointed out that most of the specimens in these two Mesozoic books by the author, of which this is the second, fall into the E through G ranges and that this is after preparation, which is usually time consuming.

The value range for fossils illustrated in this book:

A: $1,000-$2,000
B: $500-$1,000
C: $250-$500
D: $100-$250
E: $50-$100
F: $25-$50
G: $10-$25
H: $1-$10

Library of Congress Control Number: 2008936057

Designed by Mark David Bowyer
Type set in Bodoni Bd BT / Zurich BT

ISBN: 978-0-7643-3259-3
Printed in China

Schiffer Books are available at special discounts for bulk purchases for sales promotions or premiums. Special editions, including personalized covers, corporate imprints, and excerpts can be created in large quantities for special needs. For more information contact the publisher:

Published by Schiffer Publishing Ltd.
4880 Lower Valley Road
Atglen, PA 19310
Phone: (610) 593-1777; Fax: (610) 593-2002
E-mail: Info@schifferbooks.com

For the largest selection of fine reference books on this and related subjects, please visit our web site at
www.schifferbooks.com
We are always looking for people to write books on new and related subjects. If you have an idea for a book please contact us at the above address.

This book may be purchased from the publisher.
Include $5.00 for shipping.
Please try your bookstore first.
You may write for a free catalog.

In Europe, Schiffer books are distributed by
Bushwood Books
6 Marksbury Ave.
Kew Gardens
Surrey TW9 4JF England
Phone: 44 (0) 20 8392 8585; Fax: 44 (0) 20 8392 9876
E-mail: info@bushwoodbooks.co.uk
Website: www.bushwoodbooks.co.uk

With regards,
Bruce L. Stinchcomb

Contents

Acknowledgments

Acknowledgement is made to the following for their involvement in various ways with Cretaceous rocks and their fossils: Chris Baught, William Brownfield, Carl Campbell, Dorothy Echols, Patricia Eicks, Don Frizzell, Mike Fix, Matthew Forir, Guy Darrough, John McLeod, Curvin Metzler, John Stade, Elizabeth Stinchcomb, and Warren Wagner.

Last but not least, special thanks to my parents, Leonard and Virginia Stinchcomb, for encouraging my strong interest in fossils at an early age, and—specifically with regard to the subject of this book—for introducing me to rocks and fossils of the Cretaceous while enduring the summer heat of northern Mississippi at the Owl Creek type locality as well as other Cretaceous localities in western Tennessee (Coon Creek) and Missouri (Ardeola).

Introduction

As a direct record of life on the earth through the course of megatime, **fossils** offer a **collectable** which is rich in **scientific significance**. These "***medals of creation***" offer a tangible record of the changes in life over four billion years of the fifteen billion years since the **Big Bang**. This book, the fourth in a series with a bent toward the collector, provides – like the author's previous books, *Worlds Oldest Fossils, Paleozoic Fossils, and Mesozoic Fossils-I* – "eye candy" to the fossil collector as well as fascinating objects to any person curious about the great swell of life preceding the appearance of man.

Fossils presented in these four books offer a record of life over one quarter of the time since the Big Bang, fifteen billion years ago. If, as quantum physics suggests, the Universe did not exist until an intelligent observer came onto the scene ("humanity made the Universe conscious of itself"), fossils represent tangible "artifacts" representing that life which appeared prior to human evolution and can now be "seen" by humanity. What is seen on the third planet from the Sun is a quirky and erratic "parade" of life in ever-increasing diversity, preserved in the rocks of this planet as fossils. These fossils become greater in diversity the closer one comes to the present age. The **Cretaceous**, a small speck of time just before the bottom of the eye of the intelligent observer in the diagram of the Big Bang represents a quantum leap in biogenic diversity before the Cenozoic Era, the Cenozoic Era being the era that saw the modern world, as we know it, unfold and evolve, complete with the appearance of human intelligence.

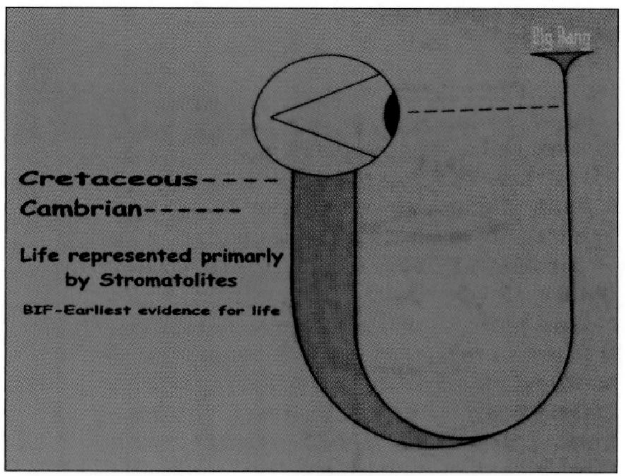

Chapter One

The Cretaceous Period

The Cretaceous Period, the youngest period of the Mesozoic Era, gets its name from the frequent occurrence of chalk (Latin – *Creta* = chalk) found in strata of this time period—strata deposited during the time span from 120 million years ago to 67 million years ago.

Specifically the Cretaceous period was named after **chalk** exposed in the sea cliffs of southern England along the English Channel (The white cliffs of Dover) as well as in other parts of Europe like the Netherlands, Denmark, France, and even the Mediterranean. Chalk represents biochemical sediment composed of small particles of calcium carbonate, much of it of organic origin (Coccoliths and Rhabdoliths). Curiously, in the nineteenth century a controversy existed over whether the soft limestone of North America was really true chalk! Many geologists of that time insisting that true chalk was to be found only in Europe and that the chalk of Kansas and Alabama was really soft limestone (which is what chalk is!).

Why does this book deal with only one geologic period, a period that was named after *chalk*? Originally it was planned to have a single book dealing entirely with Mesozoic fossils with a focus on collecting. This was to be based on a specific portion of geologic time, as were previous works in the series: *The World's Oldest Fossils* and **Paleozoic Fossils**. Like the previous works, this Mesozoic book would focus upon those fossils that are available to collectors as well as those which were available to the author. As the diversity, availability, and abundance of fossils increases the closer one gets to the present (in part as a function of the increased diversity of life itself), there seemed to be an amount of material too great to be included in a single book without creating a truly voluminous work. At a certain point it was found necessary to divide the Mesozoic into two books to accommodate that wealth of fossils available, thereby poignantly expressing the diversity of Mesozoic life. With the current arrangement, fossils of the Mesozoic Era are divided into two volumes: book one—Fossils of the Triassic and Jurassic Periods and book two, this one—Fossils of the Cretaceous Period. With this arrangement, widespread and fossil-rich Cretaceous strata could be represented on a scale comparable with that of previous books in the series.

Figure 01-001. Chalk is the distinctive rock of the Cretaceous Period of the Mesozoic Era; it is the rock for which the Cretaceous is named; Creta (L)=chalk. Chalk outcrops in England, Holland, and Denmark were the original areas of outcrop which formed this namesake of the Cretaceous, the third and last period of the Mesozoic Era. This is a Late Cretaceous chalk outcrop in western Kansas (Niobara Chalk).

Figure 01-002. The Niobara Chalk (chalk outcrop), well exposed in western Kansas in an arid environment.

Figure 01-003. Chalky shale or chalky mudstone is more characteristic of Cretaceous strata in many parts of the world than is chalk. These chalky mudstones (marl), in southern Arkansas, contain numerous fossil oysters. In a humid climate like that of the southeastern U.S., such outcrops tend to grow over quickly; this outcrop no longer looks like this.

Figure 01-004. Chalky limestone and marl (soft, impure limestone) was exposed in an excavation near Tupelo, Mississippi, in the early 1960s. This outcrop, like many in soft, friable rocks, no longer exists. The site was just east of the boyhood home of popular music icon Elvis Presley and is now occupied by a car dealership.

The Cretaceous is the youngest period of the Mesozoic Era, the "**Age of Reptiles**." The earliest part of that period finds the transition from Jurassic life forms like ammonites and belemnites changing in subtle ways; however the Jurassic-Cretaceous boundary is a "soft" one, being represented by a gradual transition in its fossils in contrast to those found at the end of the Cretaceous, with its many extinctions. In other words, fossils of the Jurassic Period grade into those of the Cretaceous; there is no "hard" or abrupt boundary like that found at the end of the Cretaceous. The "hard" boundary at the end of the Cretaceous is one of the fossil record's most abrupt, being marked by the extinction of numerous life forms; life forms which include such well established groups as ammonites and belemnites as well as many microfossils, a category of fossils which are not represented in this work. Extinction of numerous vertebrate groups, which include the dinosaurs, mimics this sudden and widespread extinction. In fact, the original recognition of the end of the Cretaceous was at least, in part, delineated by recognition of the extinction of dinosaurs, Mosasaurs, and other ruling reptiles.

Reasons for the sudden demise of many life forms at the end of the Cretaceous has been debated since it was first recognized in the early nineteenth century. Explanations for these extinctions have been numerous, including the rise of angiosperms (their alkaloids poisoned the dinosaurs), increased tectonic activity and accompanying climate change as well as racial or taxonomic senility (with the ammonites). Extra Solar System phenomena—like a nearby supernova in our part of the Milky Way Galaxy—has even been suggested. In fact it was a search for isotopic signatures—signatures which may have been produced by such a supernova—that led to the discovery of a worldwide concentration of the element iridium at the Cretaceous-Tertiary (K/T) boundary, a clue to the phenomena which may have given rise to at least part, if not all, of the extinctions.

Figure 01-005. Grey shale like this is typical of Cretaceous rocks of western North America. These thick shales and interbedded sandstones are usually not fossiliferous (fossil bearing) as are Cretaceous rocks in the southeastern part of North America. A seaway (the North American Mediterranean) split North America into two parts during the Late Cretaceous. These grey, marine shales exposed along the Cheyenne River of South Dakota, contain marine fossils like ammonites and *Inoceramus* clams.

Iridium is a component of many meteorites and their parent asteroids. A concentration of iridium, the iridium "spike" discovered at the K/T boundary, has been associated with the impact and vaporization of an asteroid(s) that hit the Earth sixty-seven million years ago. Worldwide ecological disruptions from dust ejected into the stratosphere from this event, as well as other catastrophic effects of such an impact, are offered as causes for the massive extinctions at the K/T boundary. Impact glass found at the Cretaceous-Tertiary boundary (K/T boundary) in exploratory drilling for petroleum in the Yucatan Peninsula in the southern Gulf of Mexico region suggests that a massive impact took place in that region at the time of the extinctions. This sizeable structure, almost certainly of impact origin found by petroleum exploration, zeroed in on where such an asteroid might have impacted and is referred to as the Chicxalub impact structure, a "handle" derived from a nearby Mexican town of that name. As the impact took place at the margin of the Gulf of Mexico, a huge tsunami is believed to have been generated from it. Evidence for this mega-tsunami exists in strata of various parts of the Gulf region, including the northern Gulf region, now some 500 miles from the present Gulf of Mexico.

Figure 01-006. Upper Cretaceous marine shale and sandstone, southern Utah.

Figure 01-007. Strata at the top of the Cretaceous are exposed in the road cut to the right. Overlying sandstone and mudstone beds are Paleocene in age (Fort Union Group). The K/T boundary is shown in the road cut. Hills in the distance are made up of uranium bearing Cenozoic strata (Wasatch Group). Rattlesnake Range, central Wyoming.

Collecting Cretaceous Fossils

Strata of the Cretaceous yield some of the most diverse and accessible fossils of any part of geologic time. Its fossils have often been the basis for creating many fossil collectors and aficionados—persons who have then pursued science in one way or another as a consequence of the ***science-fiction-like*** nature and yet ***hands-on*** accessibility of these fossils.

Cretaceous rocks can be a rich source of accessible and nice fossils! Fossils offer an enticing pathway for persons to become interested in paleontology, with its various connections to geology, biology, and even chemistry and physics. Fossils are great in that they can offer a "hands on" vehicle, which can form the nucleus of a person's sincere interest in science.

It is with the above in mind that the author finds it puzzling to encounter, sometimes within paleontology itself, persons who bemoan the collector. Fossils, besides being scientifically related objects, are often objects of beauty—a concept which appears to be lost on some of those "totally scientifically oriented" individuals, who loath collectors and have had considerable influence in industry or government.

The author once encountered at a fossil fair (MAPS EXPO) a cadre of such persons who had an obvious disdain for the entire fair. After hearing criticism regarding the inclusion of many of the fossils of the fair and the inappropriateness of collecting them, the author pointed out some nearby Cretaceous vertebrate fossils at a dealer's stand that came from phosphate pits in Morocco. The author mentioned that such fossils would go through a rock crusher if they had not been "collected." One of the cadres members came back with the terse rebuttal that "such material didn't have **stratigraphic documentation** and with out it such fossils were **worthless."** While this point of view is narrowly correct as these objects have been removed from their strata and have lost much valuable data concerning their associations with other fossils and the environment of that age, it is a bit of an overstatement to suggest such fossils are absolutely worthless. Such a mindset gives no consideration to the aesthetic or educational value of fossils. Science with such a clinical attitude turns off many otherwise sympathetic persons and this attitude is detrimental not only to paleontology itself, but to science in general. As an extension on this point, probably nowhere is this mindset currently more devastating to science than it is in the space program. The somewhat frequently heard objection to a manned space program—an objection sometimes heard coming from scientists—like the disregard for the Moroccan mosasaur fossils—negates the romantic aspects of manned space exploration and looks only at such exploration as a medium for the gathering of scientific data. The public at large is **not** going to be enthralled at spending public money on a space program *exclusively* for the gathering of scientific data and it is the public which, through its governmental agents, and not scientists, who will ultimately determine the fate of the program. In the same manner, a lot of people *like* fossils (isn't that why you're reading this book?), so paleontologists should recognize, cultivate such interest, and work constructively with the broader community of enthusiasts so that both may gain from the exchange of information and association, and not try to discourage it.

Figure 01-008. Late Cretaceous, Pierre Shale exposed in the center of Teapot Dome, north of Casper, Wyoming. Hills in the distance are composed of uppermost Cretaceous rocks (Lance Formation), which has been removed by erosion in the foreground, removed by erosion from the uplifted part of Teapot Dome. Beds of volcanic ash or bentonite outcrop in the vicinity of the oil pumps.

Figure 01-009. Teapot Dome oil field, Wyoming, with late Cretaceous shales (Pierre or Bearpaw shale) at the surface. The Teapot Dome oilfield was the subject of a political scandal in the early 1920s during the Harding administration. The petroleum comes from Paleozoic strata at a depth of some 12,000 feet.

Figure 01-010. The Mesa Verde Sandstone at Mesa Verde, Colorado. This thick sandstone forms the top of Upper Cretaceous (and Mesozoic Era) strata in the southwestern U.S.

Figure 01-011. Late Cretaceous strata near Grand Junction, Colorado (Mesa Verde Sandstone underlain by Mancos Shale).

Figure 01-012. Road cut in slabby Cretaceous limestone north of Monterrey, Mexico. Such slabby beds (at times) can be the source of excellent fossils, sometimes representing part of a "conservatat lageratatte" or paleontological window on the past. Sometimes such layers are not obviously fossiliferous, the fossils turning up only when such rock is quarried in quantity for its slabs used for building purposes.

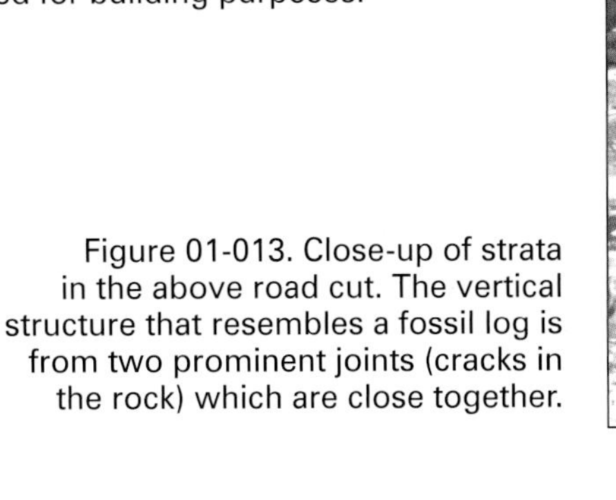

Figure 01-013. Close-up of strata in the above road cut. The vertical structure that resembles a fossil log is from two prominent joints (cracks in the rock) which are close together.

Some Peculiar Aspects of Cretaceous Age Strata

Besides extinctions at the end of the Cretaceous, the period in many parts of the world is marked by extensive igneous activity (activity associated with volcanoes and volcanism) or by igneous activity produced on a scale greater than that from any other part of geologic time since the Precambrian. Accompanying or following this igneous activity was also a time of intense worldwide tectonic activity, which saw the initial stages of tectonism—tectonism that created many of the world's mountain ranges like the Rockies, the Andes, and the Caucasus. Cretaceous rocks are some of the most widespread rock strata of any part of geologic time, and the Cretaceous has both marine and non-marine strata represented worldwide. The Cretaceous is also the earliest period that has its sediments still extensively present on the modern ocean floor; sediments of earlier geologic periods having been through the process of subduction, in which one geologic plate has been forced beneath another, and thus removed from the oceans floor. (The oldest seafloor sediments that still reside on the sea floor are of Jurassic age in the Pacific, but they are of limited occurrence and are now covered by a considerable thickness of younger sediments.) Earlier sediments are known only from where they have been piled onto the edge of continents through sea floor spreading or are represented by those sediments deposited where oceans once extensively overlapped onto the continental crust. The Cretaceous also appears to have been a period of earth history where the mid-oceanic ridges were particularly active—so that these expanded ridges displaced a considerable volume of sea water, which then spread over parts of the continents. The end of the Mesozoic Era saw a level of increased igneous activity at spreading centers of the world's oceans. These increased rates of magma extrusion, originally extruded at the mid-oceanic ridges, created sea floor basalts at a greater rate than those found during other parts of geologic time. This major increase in mid-oceanic ridge igneous activity raised ocean floors worldwide, displacing vast quantities of water. This displaced sea water then spilled onto the edges of the continents, where sediments then accumulated on these edges because of the higher sea levels. This phenomenon explains why Cretaceous age sediments cover more of the edges of the continents than do those of earlier periods of geologic time.

Cretaceous Igneous Activity and Mountain Building

As witness to enhanced igneous activity, Cretaceous rocks, particularly those of the Upper Cretaceous, often exhibit evidence of volcanic activity even in areas that today are far removed from any volcanoes. This evidence is present in the form of volcanic ash beds or vocanoclastic sediments. Less commonly, actual lava flows are interbedded with Cretaceous age strata and intrusions of igneous rocks of Cretaceous age are relatively widespread.

Figure 01-014. Thick Cretaceous shale exposed in a cirque in southern British Columbia. Thick shale sequences such as this can be sparse in their offerings of fossils as the clay (which became shale) was deposited too rapidly and in water too deep for organisms to have lived in large numbers and preserved as fossils.

Figure 01-015. Uppermost Cretaceous (Maastrichtian) coal bearing strata exposed along I-70, central Utah. The black layer is a coal seam.

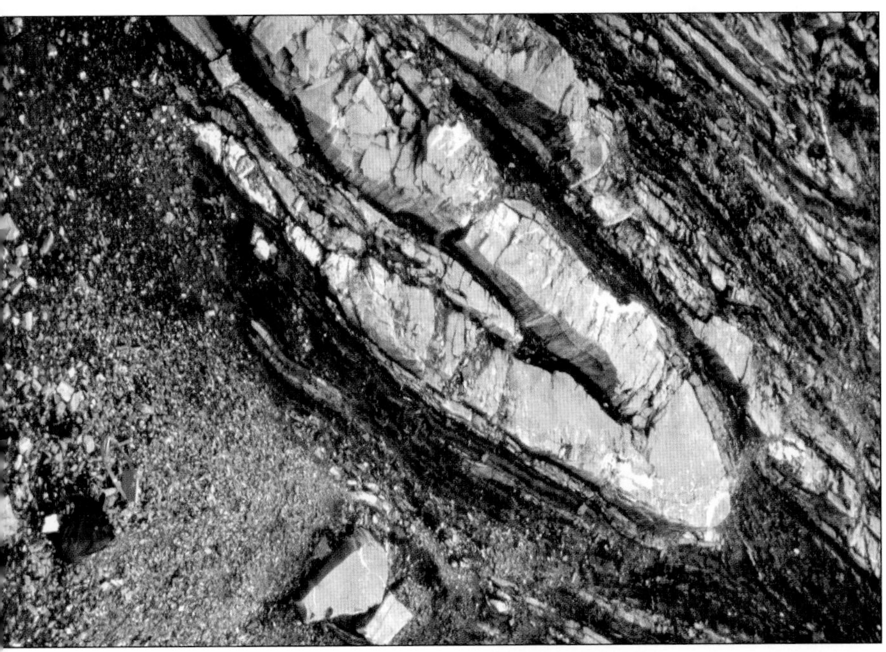

Figure 01-016. Deep sea, geosynclinal Cretaceous age strata which has been highly folded, central Alaska. Such thick, deep-sea sediments were probably scraped from the floor of the Pacific Ocean and added to the North American continent a few tens of millions of years ago. Originally from sediments of the deep ocean, such rocks are sparse in fossils and those fossils present are usually difficult to see and collect, partially as a consequence of the intense folding which these sediments have undergone.

Figure 01-017. Highly folded, deep sea Cretaceous strata exposed along the Little Tonzona River in central Alaska north of the Alaskan Range.

Figure 01-018. This soft, fossiliferous limestone (Austin Stone) of late Cretaceous age is cut and used as internal or external facing as shown here. The dark splotches are poorly preserved impressions of pelecypods (*Trigonia*).

Figure 01-019. An igneous intrusion (area where the truck is) which is parallel with and intruded into vertical layers of much older sedimentary rock during the Laramide Revolution of the late Cretaceous or early Cenozoic. The rock layers (mid-Precambrian Belt Series) that have been intruded are much older than the granite intrusion itself, which is Cretaceous in age (80 million years old).

Figure 01-020. Granite of late Mesozoic age which was intruded during the Sierra Nevada Orogeny, southern California.

Figure 01-021. Another view of granite boulders weathered from granite which was intruded during the Sierra Nevada Orogeny, southern California. Both extensive igneous activity and tectonic activity characterized the end of the Mesozoic Era.

Figure 01-022. Fossiliferous mudstone (Owl Creek Formation) in southeast Missouri. Volcanic ash is a component of these Cretaceous mudstones, a characteristic of Cretaceous rocks in many parts of the world.

Figure 01-023. The Mesozoic-Cenozoic boundary occurs about midway on this hill, below the prominent dark layer (lignitic clay) of the early Cenozoic (Paleocene) Fort Union Formation. Outcrops in the foreground are dinosaur-bearing clays of the Hell Creek Formation. The outcrop is near Jordan, Montana. *Courtesy of Carl Campbell and Paleotrek.*

Eon	Era	Period	Age my.
PHANEROZOIC	Cenozoic		0
		Tertiary	67
	Mesozoic	Cretaceous	
		Jurassic	
		Triassic	235
	Paleozoic	Permian	280
		Pennsylvanian	
		Mississippian	300
		Devonian	350
		Silurian	320
		Ordovician	440
		[illegible]	500
		Cambrian	542
Precambrian ↓			

Figure 01-024. The Mesozoic Era relative to the Phanerozoic—that part of geologic time where fossils are obvious and often abundant.

Eon	Era	Period	Epoch	Age	Age my.
PHANEROZOIC				Present	0
	Cenozoic	Quaternary	Neogene	Holocene	
				Pleistocene	
		Tertiary		Pliocene	
				Miocene	
			Paleogene	Oligocene	
				Eocene	
				Paleocene	
					67 K/T extinctions
	Mesozoic	Cretaceous	Upper Cretaceous	Maastrichtian	
				Campanian	
				Santonian	
				Coniacian	
				Turonian	
				Cenomanian	
			Lower Cretaceous	Albian	
				Aptian	
				Neocomian	
		Jurassic			
		Triassic			
	Paleozoic				

Figure 01-025. The Cretaceous (green) in relationship to the Mesozoic and Cenozoic Eras. The series of the Cretaceous are shown, Neocomian through Maastrichtian. The Maastrichtian usually ends the Cretaceous period. The Tertiary constitutes most of the Cenozoic Era.

Early workers in the nineteenth century dealing with Cretaceous age rocks observing this presence of igneous phenomena in Cretaceous strata offered an interesting explanation of Cretaceous life relative to it—an explanation which particularly concerned occurrences of the ruling reptiles. The suggestion was that during the Mesozoic, the earth was warmer than it is today, for during the Mesozoic it hadn't yet **totally cooled** and cold-blooded animals, like dinosaurs and mosasaurs, had a physiology ideally suited for this warmer earth. With the cooling of the earth, after the Mesozoic Era, warm-blooded mammals became the more appropriate design. These early workers explained such physiological adaptation for living in a warmer Mesozoic Era as the design of an omnipotent God as the proponents of this idea were creationists and "men of the cloth" such as William Buckland and Edward Hitchcock—even Charles Lyell, often considered as the founder of modern geology, entertained this idea, at least in his earlier writings.

Cretaceous Lagerstatte and Significant Faunas

Cretaceous strata is the host rock for a number of exceptional "windows" on the geologic past (lagerstatte) which are found at various places around the globe. The fish-bearing concretions of the Santana Formation of the Arraripe Plateau of northeast Brazil and the related Crato Formation with its extensive fossil insects being two examples. On the opposite side of the globe is the Lower Cretaceous lagoonal limestone of Lebanon with its exceptional marine fossils, a sort of Cretaceous "Solnhofen-like" occurrence. Lake deposits preserving a variety of fossil vertebrates, including toothed birds, occur in Loaning Province of northeast China (although these deposits are partially of Jurassic age).

The mid-Upper Cretaceous Niobara Chalk of western Kansas, Colorado, and other states and provinces of the North American high plains is a source for spectacular fossil fish, marine reptiles, and pterosaurs. Lower Cretaceous marine strata like the Duck Creek and Glen Rose limestone deposits of Texas yield marine faunas somewhat suggestive of the Jurassic Period, and non-marine shale and sandstone on many continents yield extensive dinosaur faunas—faunas like those of the Hell Creek Formation of Montana and Alberta and even those of the north slope of Alaska. More related to personal fossil collecting are the fine marine invertebrates of the Pierre and Bearpaw shale of the North American high plains. The overlying Fox Hills sandstone in parts of the same region is also a source of spectacular ammonites and other mollusks. Upper Cretaceous phosphate rock mined in southwestern Morocco has been a source for spectacular vertebrates, specifically Mosasaurs, Plesiosaurs, crocodilians, and shark's teeth.

Other notable Cretaceous fossil occurrences illustrated in this work are the extensive invertebrate faunas of the Owl Creek and Coon Creek Formations and their correlatives in Tennessee, Mississippi, Missouri, Arkansas, and Texas. These deposits yield one of the most diverse Cretaceous molluscan faunas known. Also worthy of mention are the dinosaur eggs (Therizinosaur) of Hubei Province, China, and the peculiar silicified dinosaur eggs of Argentina. Cretaceous strata of Europe, the far western U. S., Alaska, Morocco, and Madagascar yield a variety of fine and widely distributed ammonites.

In addition to the above mentioned occurrences, Cretaceous rocks worldwide offer opportunities to obtain diverse and exceptional fossils from a variety of environments, including normal marine, brackish water, lacaustrian (lake), and terrestrial environments. The reason for such a diversity of fossils representative of such different environments comes from the worldwide extent and fossil-rich nature of Cretaceous age rocks and strata. It is interesting to contemplate, in light of the wide extent of Cretaceous rocks, what new fossils and faunas of this age will turn up in the future.

Bibliography

Alvarez, Luis, Walter Alvarez, Franke Asaro, and Helen V. Michel, 1980. "Extraterrestrial cause for the Cretaceous-Tertiary extinctions." *Science* v. 208, pg. 1095-0116.

Campbell, Carl E., and Francisca E. Oboh-Ikuenobe, 2008. "Megatsunami deposit in Cretaceous-Paleogene boundary interval of southeastern Missouri." *Geological Society of America, Special Paper* 437. Geological Society of America, Denver.

Psihoyos, Louie and John Knoebber, 1994. *Hunting Dinosaurs*. Random House, New York.

Sohl, Norman F. and Earle G Kauffman, 1964. "Giant Upper Cretaceous Oysters from the Gulf Coast and Caribbean." *U. S. Geological Survey Professional Paper* 483-H U. S. Government Printing Office, Washington D. C.

Willford, John Noble, 11986. *The Riddle of the Dinosaur*. Alfred A. Knopf, New York.

Chapter Two

The Lower (Early) Cretaceous

The Earliest Part of the Last Period of the Mesozoic Era

The earliest part of the Cretaceous Period (or the Lower Cretaceous) has been recognized since the mid-nineteenth century as different in its fossil content from strata of the later or younger part of the Cretaceous. This paleontological distinctiveness led to a proposal early in the twentieth century to erect another geologic period in the Mesozoic Era, a period between the Jurassic and the Upper Cretaceous periods to be called the **Comanchean**. This proposal would have given four periods to the Mesozoic: the Triassic, Jurassic, **Comanchean,** and the Cretaceous. Concurrent with this revision of the geologic time scale was a proposal to add two periods between the Cambrian and the Ordovician, the Ozarkian and Canadian Periods. A decade earlier, the Mississippian and Pennsylvanian periods had been proposed and substituted for the European Carboniferous so such revisions were "in the air" and were reasonable for the time. As with the Ozarkian and Canadian periods, this revision was proposed as the fossils of the Lower Cretaceous are in many ways quite distinctive from those of the Upper Cretaceous. The demise of these proposals was more a consequence of mental inertia and geological and paleontological politics of the time than anything else. It wasn't that they were not valid, as parts of the geologic time scale are somewhat arbitrary anyway and the fossils of the Comanchean really **are distinctive** from those of the "real" Cretaceous, that is the Upper Cretaceous ... and its chalk.

It should also be noted that most textbooks don't have a middle Cretaceous, only a Lower and an Upper part to the period. Other geologic periods have a three-part, lower, middle, and upper division to them. This is again a consequence of the **lower** part of that sequence of rock strata, designated as Lower Cretaceous, being distinctive and standing out paleontologically from the rest of the period.

Figure 02-001. *Osmundia* sp. This fern is from Lower Cretaceous strata associated with a peculiar tree fern known as *Tempskyia* sp. Wayan, southern Idaho. (Value range F).

Plants

Early Cretaceous plants resemble those of the Jurassic, there were **few** flowering plants (angiosperms) at this time. Lower Cretaceous plants, in part, consisted of a variety of tree ferns like these.

Figure 02-002. Another example of what is probably the foliage of a tree fern, Wayan, southern Idaho. (Value range F).

Figure 02-003. *Osmundia* sp. Foliage of a tree fern.

Figure 02-004. *Anemia* sp. This distinctive foliage is believed to have been that of the peculiar Mesozoic tree known as *Tempskyia*. Petrified logs of *Tempskyia* occur in Cretaceous strata, particularly in Idaho and British Columbia, Canada.

Figure 02-005. A group of small specimens of *Anemia* sp., believed to be the foliage of *Tempskyia*. Wayan, Idaho.

Figure 02-006. *Tempskyia* sp. A cross section of the "trunk" of this peculiar early Cretaceous tree fern showing bundles of the small roots which make up its large "trunk." Wayan, Idaho. (Value range E).

Conifers of various types, like these, were dominant Lower Cretaceous plants.

Figure 02-007. Right: *Metasequoia* sp.; Left: *Taxodium*, Smithers, British Columbia. Large forests of primitive conifers, which included Sequoia, Metasequoia, and Taxodium (Cypress), existed during the Cretaceous and the early Cenozoic. It's often difficult to distinguish these different conifer genera from each other, particularly with regard to specimens preserving young leaves verses old ones. These two leaf types display the maximum differences between *Metasequoia* and *Taxodium*. Tuffaceous (volcanic ash-rich) shales near Smithers, British Columbia. *Courtesy of Raymond Lasmanis.* (Value range F, single specimen)

Figure 02-008. *Taxodium* sp. This group of bald cypress leaves is preserved in a tuffaceous shale which crops out in the vicinity of Smithers, British Columbia. A partial metasequoia leaf is at the bottom. (Value range F).

Figure 02-009. *Taxodium* sp. Leaves of the bald cypress (*Taxodium*) can locally be common fossils and can be associated with *Metasequoia* from which it is sometimes difficult to distinguish. Lower Cretaceous, tuffaceous shales, Smithers, British Columbia. (Value range F)

Figure 02-010. *Metasequoia* sp. This metasequoia leaf is associated with a tuffaceous shale layer, which is full of the foliage of primitive conifers. Smithers, British Columbia, Canada. *Courtesy of Raymond Lasmanis.*

Figure 02-011. Unidentified conifer. Talkeetna Mountains, southern Alaska.

Ginko's were a locally abundant, Lower Cretaceous plant; a type of dinosaur "salad", at least for herbivorous dinosaurs.

Figure 02-012. *Ginkgo* sp. A fossil ginko leaf next to the leaf of the modern *Ginkgo biloba* (right). Ginkgos were dominant Mesozoic trees and gingko leaves and seeds were probably eaten by herbivorous dinosaurs. What are believed to be fragments of Ginkgo seeds have been found in some dinosaur coprolites. (Value range for fossil ginkgo leaf F).

Figure 02-013. *Ginkgo* sp. A group of ginkgo leaves with the modern *Ginkgo biloba* at the bottom.

Flowering plants are found in Lower Cretaceous rocks but they are rare fossils.

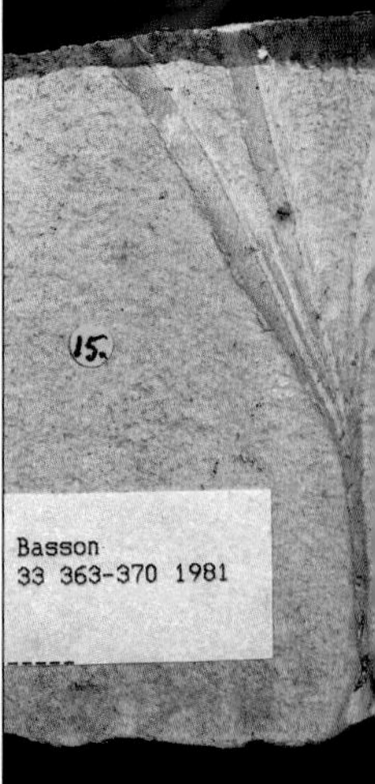

Figure 02-014. *Sapindopsis* sp. An early angiosperm impression in fine-grained limestone from one of the Early Cretaceous lagerstatte or paleontological windows in Lebanon. This is one of the earlier and primitive angiosperms in the fossil record, it comes from Cenommanian age strata, sometimes given as Middle Cretaceous. Nammoura, Lebanon. (Value range F).

Figure 02-015. *Araliopsoides cretacea*. These sassafras-like leaves came from the Dakota Sandstone of Kansas and are from a locality that yielded a large number of them in the early twentieth century as well as yielding fossil leaves which resemble a sycamore. The Dakota Sandstone varies in age from late Lower Cretaceous to early late (Upper Cretaceous). There is some doubt that these early angiosperms really represent sassafras and sycamore as pollen of both of these trees has **not** been found in rock strata anywhere close to the age of these fossils. If they were sassafras and sycamore, the distinctive pollen of these angiosperms should have been found with the leaves. These fossils may be from a family of angiosperms, possibly related to modern herbaceous plants like ginseng and represent a plant that went extinct prior to the appearance of more modern angiosperms, which appear in the late Cenozoic. Leaves like this surface in old collections but they are rarely found today. (Value range E).

Figure 02-016. This is an outcrop of the Dakota Sandstone in western Kansas. The Dakota Sandstone varies from Lower Cretaceous in Wyoming and Montana to early late Cretaceous in central Nebraska and Kansas.

These are fossil sponges. Such sponges are (or course) associated with marine sedimentary rocks.

Figure 02-017. *Raphidonema faringdonensis.* These vase-shaped calcareous sponges have been found in quantity in the lower Cretaceous age Greensand near Faringdon, Berkshire, England. This is a large specimen; most are smaller. (Value range F).

Figure 02-018. *Raphidonema faringdonensis*. A group of attractive sponge specimens from the Faringdon sponge "gravels," Faringdon, England. (Value range G, single specimen).

Echinoderms

Echinoderms in the Lower Cretaceous are well represented by sea urchins (echinoids). For reasons not understood, crinoids, sometimes quite abundant in earlier rocks, are rare in Cretaceous strata.

Figure 02-019. *Cidaris* sp. These cidarid echinoids are similar to those from the Jurassic of Germany and other parts of Europe. They come from Lower Cretaceous rocks of Morocco. (Value range F, single specimen).

Figure 02-020. *Phymosoma texanum.* A group of prepared specimens, except for the unprepared specimen at the upper right. Echinoids such as these don't look like much until they are prepared (cleaned), either by hand or by use of an air abrasive machine; both procedures can be quite time consuming, particularly with these fossils. (Value range F, single specimen).

Figure 02-021. *Selenia texana*. These cidarids can be locally abundant in the Glen Rose Formation as well as in other Lower Cretaceous limestones of Texas. Specimens from north of San Antonio, Texas. (Value range F, single prepared specimen).

Figure 02-022. *Phymosoma texanum*. These echinoids came from the Glen Rose Limestone southwest of Dallas, Texas. They have been cleaned with an air abrasive machine. (Value range F, single cleaned specimen).

Figure 02-023. *Phymosoma texanum*. A prepared specimen of this regular echinoid, which is fairly widespread in the Glen Rose Limestone of Texas.

Figure 02-024. *Micraster* sp. These are some of the earlier occurrences of irregular echinoids. They are from the Denton Limestone of Williamson Co., Texas.

Mollusks, as usual, in a marine environment are well represented as fossils by snails (gastropods) and pelecypods.

Figure 02-025. *Leptoma austinensis* Shumard. This tightly coiled gastropod can locally be a common fossil in the Duck Creek Limestone and other Comanchean limestones of central Texas. (Value range G).

Figure 02-027. A clam (pelecypod) preserved in precious opal. The opal deposits of lighting ridge in northern Australia occur in Lower Cretaceous sediments. Opalized fossils found there also include opalized plesiosaur and dinosaur bone. (Value range E).

Figure 02-026. Internal molds of a high spired, Turritella-like gastropod. Such high-spired gastropods are typical of the Cretaceous Period in many parts of the world. Atlas Mountains, Agadir, Morocco. (Value range F).

Oysters are mollusks which were particularly abundant in the Cretaceous; these are typical Lower Cretaceous forms.

Figure 02-028. *Rastellum (Alectryonia) carinata*. These are relatively small, peculiarly ornamented Lower Cretaceous oysters from the Washita Group, McLennan Co., Texas. (Value range, single specimen G).

Figure 02-029. *Gryphaea* (*Texigryphia*) *arietina*. These small, coiled oysters can be phenomenally abundant in Lower Cretaceous (Comanchean) rocks of Texas. They can be so abundant that they are sometimes dug up and used as road gravel (aggregate). Some roads in central and north central Texas are literally paved with them but when they do occur in such vast numbers, they are poorly preserved. *Courtesy of Carl J. Stinchcomb.* Comanche Peak Formation, Georgetown, Texas. (Value range G, single specimen).

Nautaloid Cephalopods

Nautaloid cephalopods, that group of mollusks represented today by the pearly nautilus of modern oceans, were widespread in the Early Cretaceous and have left a good fossil record.

Figure 02-032. *Cyamatoceras* sp. A single specimen of this attractive nautaloid from Madagascar. Such specimens have become widely distributed in rock and nature shops, they are one of the more readily available fossil nautaloid cephalopods. (Value range G).

Figure 02-030. *Cyamatoceras (Eutrephoceras) sakalavus*. These nautaloids are from Albian (Late Lower Cretaceous) strata of Madagascar where they are associated with ammonites. The genus *Eutrephoceras* sp. has a worldwide distribution like the shells of ammonites with which it is usually associated. A large number of these nautaloids have come onto the fossil market, highly polished like these specimens which show the nautaloids chambers. (Value range G, single specimen).

Figure 02-033. The same specimen of *Cyamatoceras* as in the above photo, which shows the siphuncle (hole in shell chamber). (Value range G).

Figure 02-031. *Cyamatoceras (Eutrephoceras) sakalavus*. A group of these polished, coiled nautaloids from Madagascar. The chambers of these attractive fossils are often filled with honey-yellow calcite. (Value range G, single specimen).

Figure 02-034. Another group of polished *Cyamatoceras* from the Lower Cretaceous of Madagascar.

Ammonites

Ammonites were one of the most dominant and widespread mollusks of the Cretaceous. These ammonites are some of the most beautiful and readily available ones of the entire Mesozoic Era. They are believed to have had a body similar to that of an octopus and, like the octopus, to have been fairly intelligent animals. Ammonites are beautiful and fascinating Mesozoic fossils with their complex suture patterns and shell ornamentation. The shell chambers are beautifully shown on these specimens from Madagascar.

Figure 02-036. A group of ammonites from the same locality in Peru as those in the previous photo. These ammonites, preserved in a hard, black limestone, are one of the fossils introduced in quantity onto the fossil market from Peru. They somewhat resemble the Triassic ammonites found in Nevada. Huanzala, Peru. (Value range F, single specimen).

Figure 02-035. This ammonite from Peru is similar to those from the Jurassic of Germany as well as from the Lower Cretaceous of Texas. Ammonites are cosmopolitan in their worldwide distribution as their larva could travel long distances and the ammonites themselves are believed to have been capable of traveling considerable distances. Huanzala, Peru. (Value range F).

Figure 02-037. *Desmoceras* sp. This early Cretaceous ammonite from Madagascar is similar to those of Europe; they came onto the fossil market in 2000. Ammonite faunas of the same age can be very similar over a large part of the Earth as ammonites were apparently good swimmers, their empty shells also were capable of floating long distances prior to being buried in sediments. These Lower Cretaceous ammonites from Madagascar often show beautiful shell nacre. (Average value for single specimen F).

igure 02-038. *Desmoceras* sp. Another Cretaceous mmonite from Madagascar exhibiting lustrous nacre. arge numbers of these ammonites as well as other fossils om Madagascar have entered the fossil market during the rst decade of the twenty-first century. Fossil and mineral pecimen mining (Madagascar has a wealth of beautiful ninerals as well as fossils) has been and is being done xtensively by inhabitants of this economically poor country. Most of this specimen collecting is done by hand digging. hese ammonites are dug from shale outcrops (or subcrops) n pits, which follow the ammonite bearing strata. Besides aving excellent and unique minerals, Madagascar has a ich tropical ecosystem harboring many unique species of nimals and plants. This rich ecosystem is being threatened y subsistence agriculture, which has produced severe rosion of its lateritic soils. Some environmentalists for this eason have criticized the digging of minerals and fossils for pecimen material; however, such activity is environmentally ninuscule compared to the massive removal of forests in he agricultural expansion taking place on this large island. mbarimaninga, Antananarivo Province, Madagascar. *pecimen courtesy of Stephen Riggs Jones*. (Value range F).

igure 02-039. *Cleoniceras madagascariense*. Examples of he beautiful, relatively large polished ammonites from Lower Cretaceous rocks of Madagascar. With a polished surface oth sutures and the calcite filling in the ammonite chambers ave a striking beauty. These large Madagascar ammonites are relatively inexpensive, particularly considering their eauty where they can be considered as natural *"objects de art."* Mahajanga, Madagascar. (Value range E, single specimen).

Figure 02-040. *Cleorniceras madagascariense*. A polished specimen of this relatively large ammonite with original shell nacre. (Value range E).

Figure 02-041. *Cleorniceras madagascariense*. A single, polished specimen of this beautiful ammonite. Most of the actual shell material is missing and the calcite filled interior has been polished to show the complex ammonite sutures. Mahajanga, Madagascar. (Value range E).

Figure 02-043. A nice group of various genera of polished ammonites from Madagascar. (Value range G, single specimen).

Figure 02-042. A group of small specimens of *Cleoniceras* sp. from Madagascar, which have recently (2008) become available on the fossil market. Amabarimaninga, Antananarivo Province, Madagascar. (Value range G, single specimen).

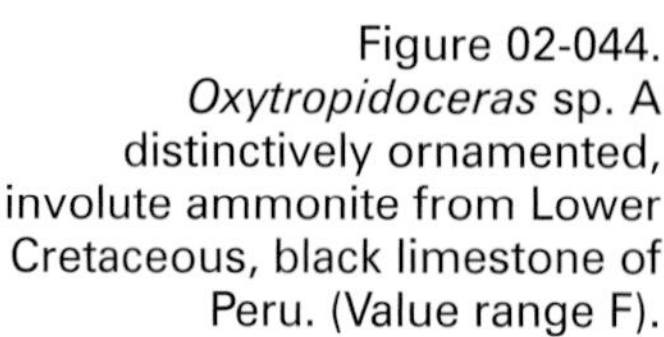

Figure 02-044. *Oxytropidoceras* sp. A distinctively ornamented, involute ammonite from Lower Cretaceous, black limestone of Peru. (Value range F).

These ammonites came from Lower Cretaceous limestone, which outcrops in central and northern Texas.

Figure 02-045. *Oxytropidoceras belknapi* Meek. Ammonite specimen from the Duck Creek Limestone, Texoma Lake, Texas. This is a common (and distinctive) Texas ammonite. (Value range E).

Figure 02-046. Two specimens of *Oxytropidoceras* from the Lower Cretaceous Duck Creek Limestone, Texoma Lake, Texas. (Value range F, single specimen).

Figure 02-047. *Oxytropidoceras* sp. A typical specimen of this ubiquitous Lower Cretaceous ammonite from the Goodland Limestone, Denton Co., Texas. *Courtesy of John McLeod*. (Value range F).

Figure 02-048. *Mortonoceras shoshonense* Meek. Well-ornamented ammonites from the Comanchean, Duck Creek Limestone of northern Texas. (Value range F).

Figure 02-049. *Mortonoceras* sp. A relatively common ammonite from the Duck Creek Limestone in the vicinity of Denison, Texas, where it is found in creek outcrops as well as along the shore of Lake Texoma on the Red River, which forms the boundary between Texas and Oklahoma. A distinctive ammonite with finely spaced ornamentation. (Value range F).

Figure 02-050. *Desmoceras brazoense* (Shumard). These large ammonites, or fragments of them, can be common fossils around Texoma Lake, Texas, as well as in other areas of north central Texas in the vicinity of Denison, Texas. (Value range F).

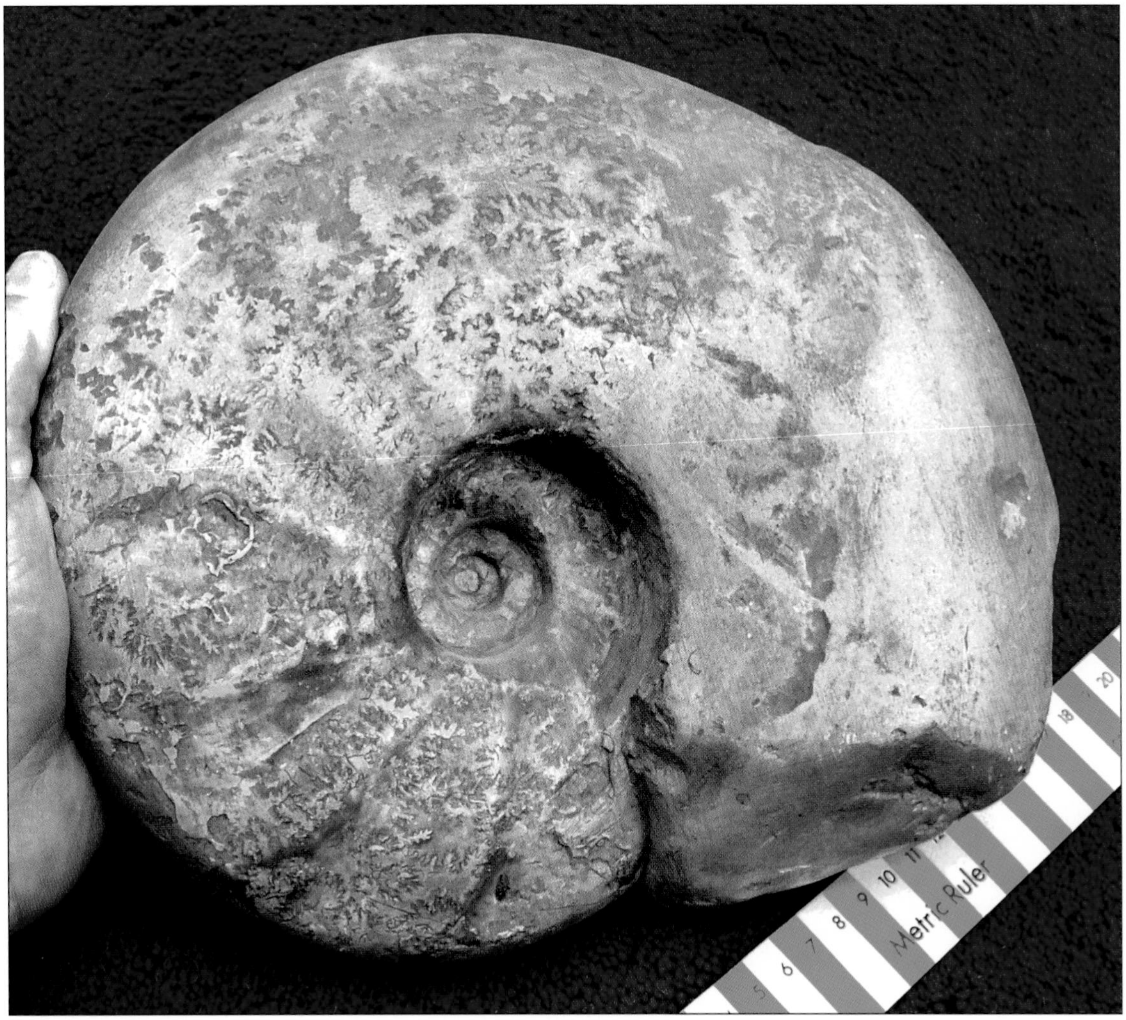

Figure 02-051. *Eopachydiscus* sp. A nice specimen of this large ammonite from the Lower Washita or Comanchean Duck Creek Limestone of northern Texas.

Figure 02-052. An ammonite of this Lower Cretaceous genus. Duck Creek Limestone, Denison, Texas.

These ammonites, from the Lower Cretaceous, have shell shapes different from the usual narrow, tight coil.

Figure 02-055. Albian ammonites from Alaska. A group of ammonites from probable deep-water sediments of the Talkeetna Mountains of southern Alaska. Cretaceous rocks of marine origin make up major parts of Alaska's mountain ranges and spectacular ammonites such as these occur locally, however their collection usually involves the traversing of a considerable amount of rough terrain of the Alaskan bush. The ammonites are (***top row***) *Lytoceras* sp., and *Freboldiceras* sp., (***middle row***), *Brewericeras* sp. and *Grantziceras* sp. (***bottom row***), *Arcthoplites* sp., *Ptychoceras* sp., and *Tetragonites* sp. Specimens collected and identified by Curvin Metzler.

Figure 02-053. These "inflated" ammonites are associated with *Cleoniceras*, the most widely distributed Madagascar ammonite. Mahajanga, Madagascar. (Value range F, single specimen).

Figure 02-054. This ammonite comes from Lower Cretaceous limestone of France. It has a distinctive morphology—morphology different from ammonites found in the Lower Cretaceous of North America.

Figure 02-056. *Phylloceras* sp. An ammonite popped from a concretion, a common occurrence of Cretaceous ammonites. Tehama County, California. *Courtesy of John McLeod*.

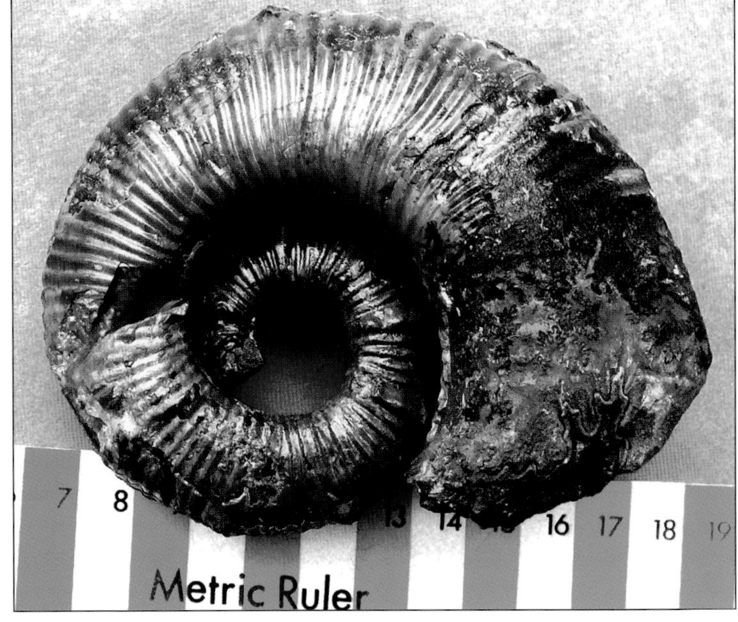

Figure 02-058. *Austraiceras jacki*. Back side of the same specimen as in the previous photo. This ammonite is peculiar in its being so loosely coiled.

Figure 02-057. *Austraiceras jacki*. A loosely coiled ammonite from Queensland, Australia. (Value range E).

Heteromorph Ammonites

Heteromorphs are peculiarly shaped ammonites which are highly collectable.

They come in a variety of shell shapes and stand out from the more "normal" planispirally coiled ammonites.

Figure 02-059. *Turrilites* sp. (*Plesioturrilites brazoensis*). *Turrilites* represents a type of ammonite known as a heteromorph. The genus *Turrilites (*or *Plesioturrilites)* resembles a high spired snail and can get quite large in the Lower Cretaceous. Heteromorphs, including *Turrilites,* are often more characteristic of the Upper Cretaceous than they are of the lower. Duck Creek Limestone, Denton, Texas. (Value range E).

Figure 02-060. *Cymatoceras sekalavus* Hyatt. A large, heteromorph ammonite from Morocco. Heteromorph ammonites are puzzling as to their mode of life. Ammonites were, like the living nautilus of today, almost certainly good swimmers but the awkward, twisted shell of many heteromorphs would have made effective movement through water difficult. Agadir, Morocco. (Value range C for a heteromorph specimen of this size).

Figure 02-061. *Glytoxoceras* sp. A disjunct (loosely coiled) heteromorph from Tehama Co., (northern) California. Ammonites found in the Cretaceous rocks of the West Coast of North America usually represent different genera than those found in the Cretaceous of the continental interior. From Tehama County, California. *Specimen courtesy of John McLeod.*

Figure 02-062. *Shastoceras shastense*. A heteromorph ammonite that resembles a (reversed) saxophone. These "saxophone" ammonites are most peculiar! Their morphology (shape) vexed some early twentieth century paleontologists as the saxophone itself was considered a lewd and licentious musical instrument—polite company didn't mention of or listen to such things. Animosity toward the saxophone was heightened by its use by minorities, who often played it with pulsating, jerky rhythms; this was particularly shocking to those raised during the late Victorian era. Fossils like this one, resembling such an immodest object, were themselves even of questionable repute. Specimen from Tehama County, California. *Courtesy of John McLeod*.

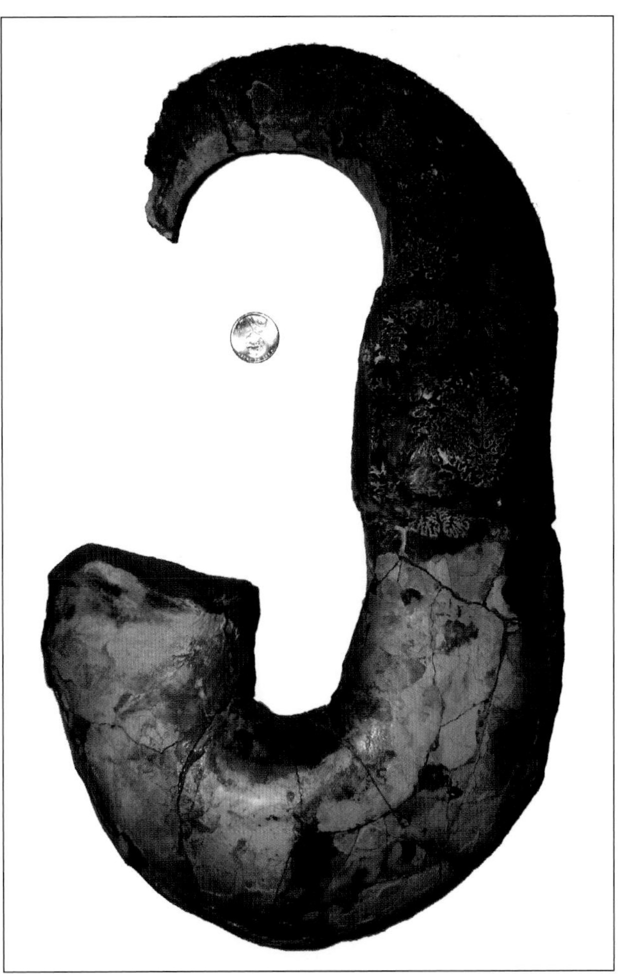

Belemnites are cephalopods believed to be related to modern squids (calamari). They can be locally abundant fossils in both Jurassic and Cretaceous strata.

Figure 02-063. *Cylindroteuthis* (*Belemnites*) sp. A belemnite from Cretaceous strata of the West Coast of North America, *Cylindroteuthis* has a vertical groove in it—like that shown in the accompanying wood cut from Charles Lyell's *Elements of Geology*. Specimens shown are from the Lower Cretaceous of northern California. (Value range G).

Arthropods

Crabs, lobsters, and shrimp can be locally found in Lower Cretaceous strata; however, they are more abundant in rocks of the Upper Cretaceous. They are covered more completely in Chapter Four.

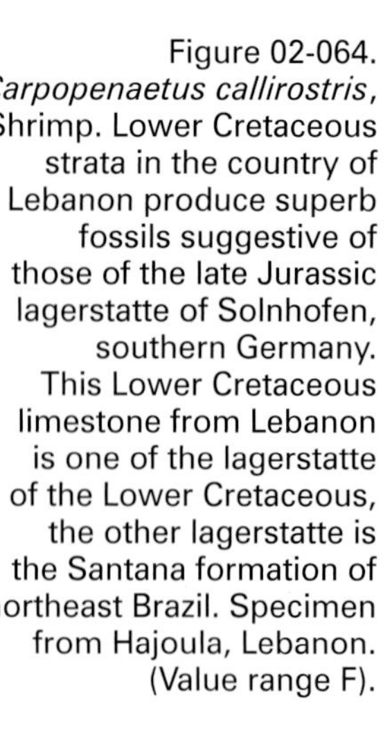

Figure 02-064. *Carpopenaetus callirostris*, Shrimp. Lower Cretaceous strata in the country of Lebanon produce superb fossils suggestive of those of the late Jurassic lagerstatte of Solnhofen, southern Germany. This Lower Cretaceous limestone from Lebanon is one of the lagerstatte of the Lower Cretaceous, the other lagerstatte is the Santana formation of northeast Brazil. Specimen from Hajoula, Lebanon. (Value range F).

Figure 02-065. *Meyerella magma*. A small lobster preserved in a concretion. Marine arthropods such as shrimp, lobsters, and crabs in the Cretaceous and Tertiary are frequently preserved in such calcareous concretions. Greensand, Isle of Wight, England (Value range F).

Figure 02-066. *Homolopsis etheridgei* (Woodward). A crab with an "Oriental face" on its carapace. Allaru Mudstone, Dartmouth, Queensland, Australia. *Courtesy of Allen Graffham of Geological Enterprises, Ardmore, Oklahoma*. (Value range F).

The following selection of fossil insects (insects are usually considered arthropods) come from Lower Cretaceous, fresh water limestone beds of northeastern Brazil. This limestone, the Crado Formation, has produced a wide variety of fossil insects—a phenomenon that usually occurs only with insects preserved in amber. The Crado Formation is a brackish water limestone, which is quarried for Portland cement and construction material. The insect fossils are recovered as a by-product of quarrying operations for this rock.

Figure 02-067. Long antenna "horned" grasshopper. Fossil insects are abundant in the Crato Member of the Santana Formation of the Araripe Plateau of Brazil. These insects are found in a fresh water limestone series, which were deposited in large, Lower Cretaceous lakes. These lake deposits have preserved vast numbers of insects and are a Lower Cretaceous paleontologic window (lagerstatten) like similar age strata of Lebanon. This is a representative of an extinct family of Cretaceous grasshoppers. (Value range F).

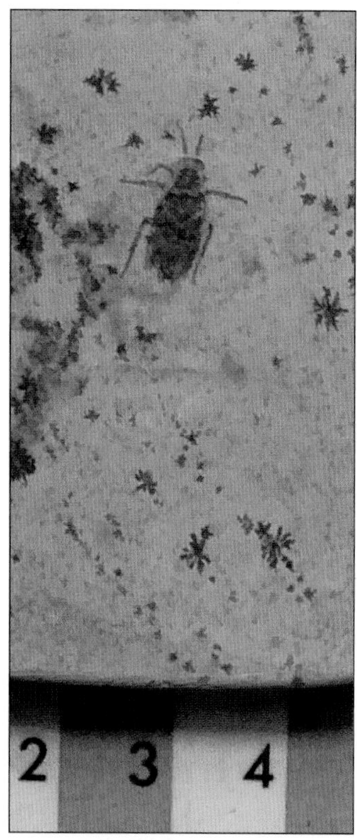

Figure 02-068. Originally identified as a **stink bug**, but probably a deformed cockroach (Blattaria).

Figure 02-069. Close up of the previous fossil. This insect from the Crato Formation (or Crato Member of the Santana Formation) is a rare fossil insect. Fossil insects this well preserved are usually associated with amber. These insects are found in a very fine grained, fresh or brackish water limestone and are preserved by being stained with a film of iron oxide.

Figure 02-070. Cockroach-1 (Blattaria). This fossil resembles a roach smashed flat on a hard surface. Its antennae are preserved and it is not much different from cockroaches of today, except for the fact that it's 125 million years old. Cockroach fossils put a different "spin" on creatures that are generally loathed by most persons. Their perseverance over long periods of geologic time (they first appear in the late Paleozoic) also puts them in a different, less loathsome light and in fact gives them somewhat of a cachet of respectability. Will we be around 125 million years in the geologic future? (Value range F).

Figure 02-071. Cockroach-2. This roach was smashed sidewise in the sediments on the lake bottom during the early Cretaceous. (Value range F).

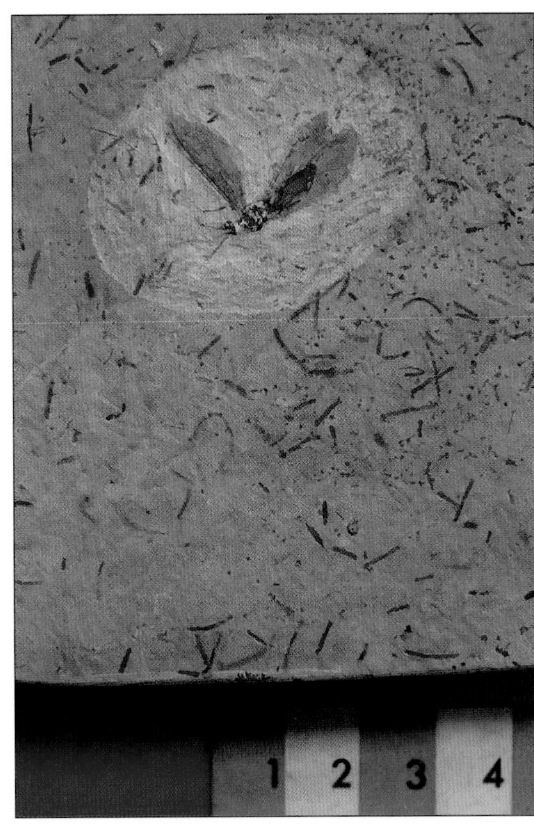

Figure 02-073. Winged termite? Winged venation indicates this is a termite (Isoptera), however, the narrow waist and large eyes suggest another affiliation. Filament-like fossils, commonly seen with these fossil insects are water plants (probably green algae), which grew in the lake where the fine sediment of the Crato Formation was being deposited. (Value range F).

Figure 02-072. Cockroach-3 Ventral view of another roach, in this case one which also was smashed (and preserved) sidewise. The vertical object is the wing of another insect. (Value range F).

Figure 02-074. Close-up of same specimen as in previous photo.

Figure 02-075. Grasshopper. An early example of a grasshopper (family Acrididae), which, however, didn't see any grass as grass (A monocot) didn't appear until much later in geologic time. (Value range F).

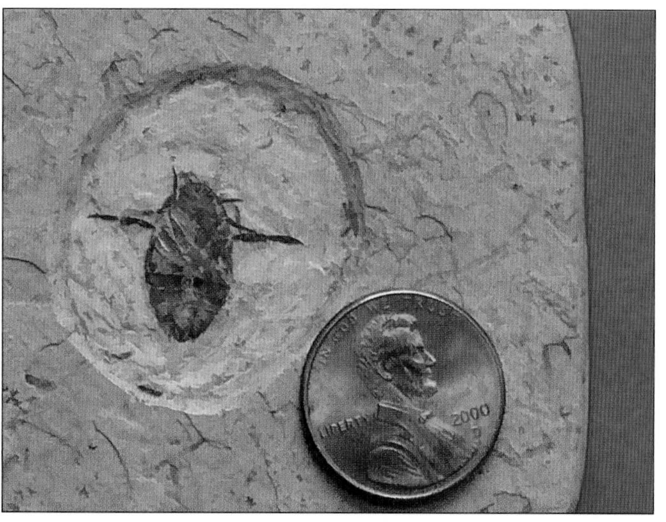

Figure 02-076. Predaceous diving beetle. The insect shown here has been exposed by carefully removing some of the enclosing limestone. The presence of these insects within the Crato Formation can be detected by the presence of slight depressions on a limestone slab. (Value range F).

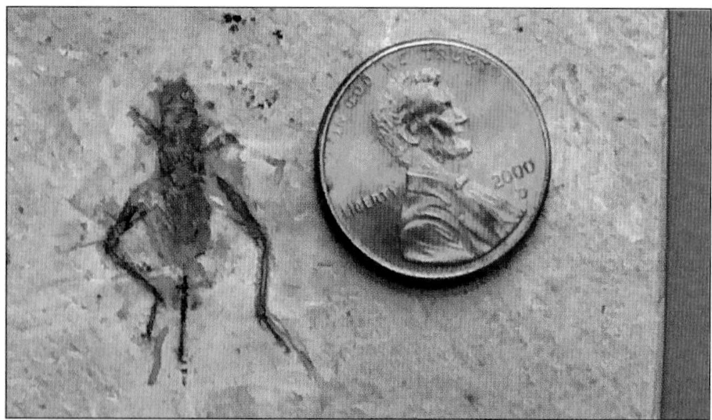

Figure 02-077. Cricket. Crickets (family Gryllidae) are known from the Jurassic Solnhofen Plattenkalk but this one from the Crato Formation is much better preserved. Insect fossils can be spectacular when preserved in brackish water lake deposits. (Value range F).

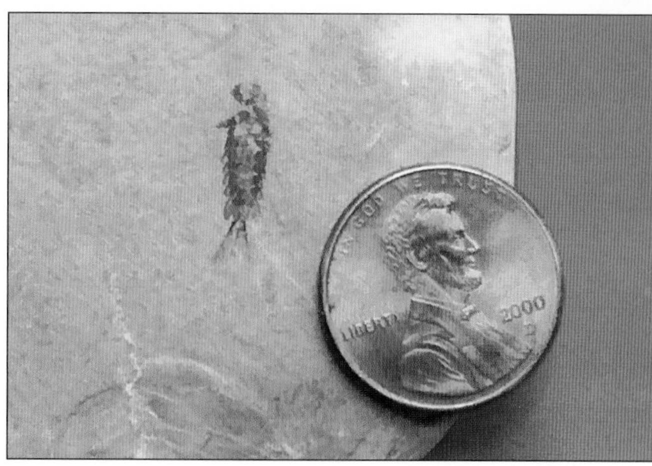

Figure 02-078. Mayfly larva. Fossils of mayfly larva similar to this are found in the similar age (Late Jurassic-Early Cretaceous) lake deposits of Liaoning Province, northeast China. This specimen is from the Crato Formation, northeast Brazil. (Value range F).

Figure 02-079. Possible bristletail larva. Crato Formation. (Value range F).

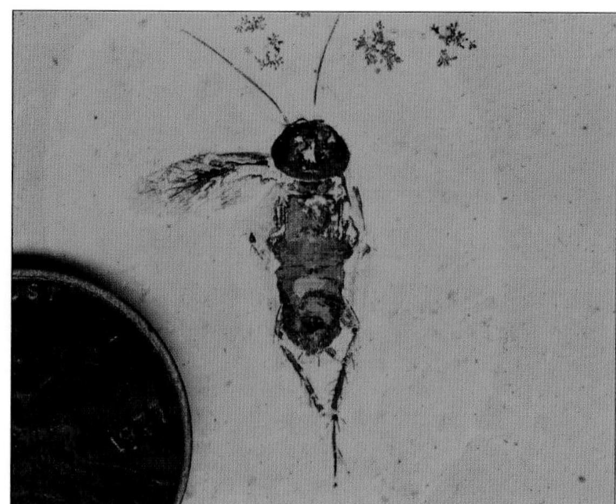

Figure 02-080. Originally thought to be a wasp—but really another cockroach. True social insects had not totally evolved in the Cretaceous; however, ancestors to them were probably around. Crado Formation. (Value range F).

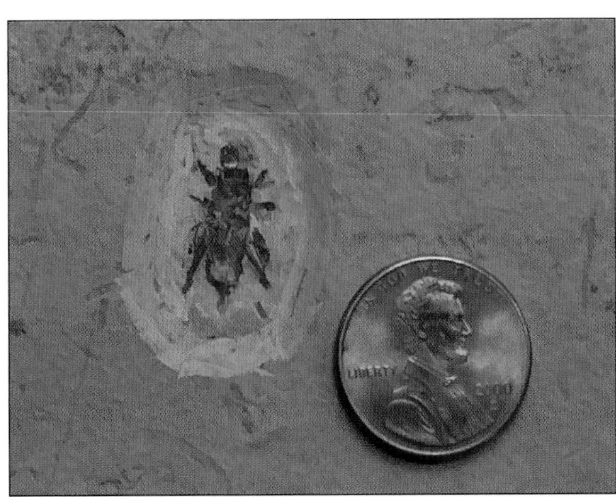

Figure 02-081. A peculiarly preserved cricket. Crado Formation, Nova Olinda Member, Araripe Plateau, Brazil.

Figure 02-082. A small fly (Diptera?) from the Crado Formation, Araripe Plateau, Brazil.

Fossil Fish

A variety of fish, including lungfish (dipnoans).

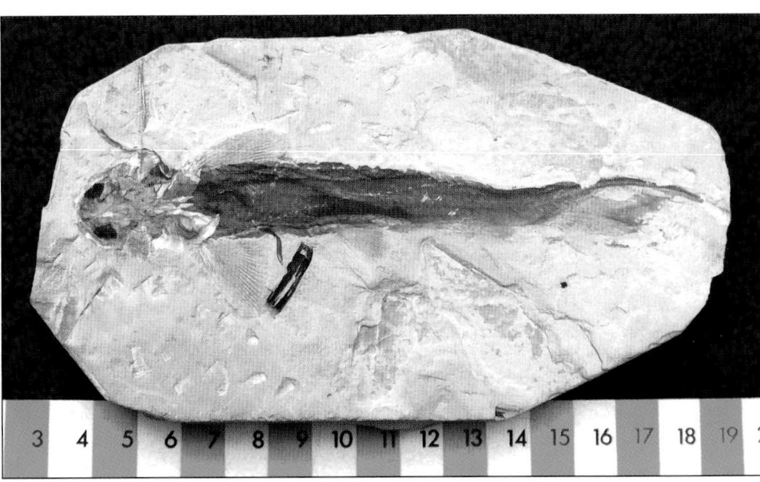

Figure 02-083. *Peipiaosteus* sp. A fossil eel. This is a fossil from the Lower Cretaceous lake deposits of Liaoning, northeastern China (Manchuria). Note the preservation of the eel's eyes! The Liaoning occurrences of fossils represent another Lower Cretaceous (and Late Jurassic) paleontologic window (lagerstatten). Jiuftang Formation, Liaoning Province (Manchuria), China. (Value range E).

Figure 02-084. *Ceratodus* sp. Toothplates of a large lungfish. Lungfish first appear in the Devonian and are still around today. During periods when the water in which they live dried up, they lived in dried mud and breath by means of a primitive lung—hence the name **lungfish**. Numerous specimens of these distinctive tooth plates have come from Libya through Moroccan fossil dealers. (Value range F, single tooth).

Figure 02-085. A complete (Devonian) lungfish (dipnoan) with tooth plates of a much larger lungfish from Libya. These lungfish teeth come from fresh water (continental) deposits of central Africa, which also yield dinosaur, crocodile, and pterodactyl teeth. Such continental deposits can span a large portion of the Cretaceous Period.

Figure 02-086. This is a highly disarticulated fish. The Mowry Formation of Wyoming can be full of scales of teleost fish like these, but complete fish fossils in this formation are almost entirely absent. Mowry Formation, Casper, Wyoming.

Figure 02-087. Another group of characteristic fish scales from the Mowry Formation, Casper, Wyoming. The scales are found over a large area and mark a horizon in the Mowry Formation that can be recognized over a large part of Wyoming and Montana. They form a marker bed that can even be identified in deep drill holes.

These fish come from early Cretaceous limestone deposited in a setting (a back reef lagoon) similar to that of the late Jurassic of Solnhofen, Germany. Like at Solnhofen, preservation of many of these fossils from Lebanon is extraordinary.

Figure 02-088. *Paleobalistum goedeli*. A wide-bodied fish from one of the Cretaceous lagerstatten of Lebanon, Hagel, Lebanon. (Value range E).

Figure 02-089. *Prionolepis cataphractus*. This is a relatively rare bony fish (teleost) from Lower Cretaceous rocks of Lebanon. Teleost (bony) fish become more abundant and diversified in the Cenozoic Era than they were in the Cretaceous. They are the most abundant and diversified fish today, being found in both marine and fresh water. This is one of the most commonly found fossils at one of the most productive Lebanese fossil sites, Hjoula, Lebanon. (Value range E).

Figure 02-090. *Exceotoides minor*. An example of one of the more common fossils from thin bedded, back reef, lagoon marine limestone at Hagel, Lebanon. (Value range F).

Figure 02-091. *Diplomystus* sp. A herring from Lower Cretaceous strata at Hagel, Lebanon.

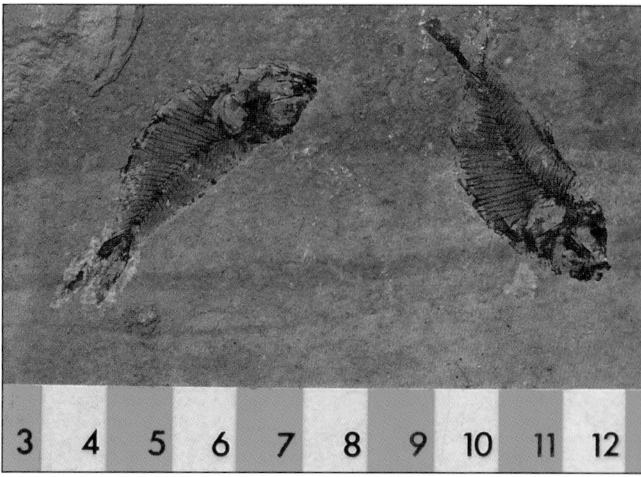

Figure 02-092. *Diplomystus* sp. (herring). Two small teleostean fish that are the most common fossil fish found at Hjoula, Lebanon. (Value range F).

Figure 02-093. A group of *Prionolepis* sp., the most common fossil fish from Hjoula, Lebanon. (Value range E).

A variety of fossil fish are known from the Lower Cretaceous Santana Formation of northeastern Brazil. Specimens of these fish, usually preserved in concretions, have been widely distributed among collectors, both institutional and private individuals alike.

Figure 02-094. *Belonostomus (Vinctifer) comptoni*. A particularly long, primitive teleost fish, which is one of the most common fish of the Santana Formation. The Santana Formation is a brackish or fresh water Lower Cretaceous sequence that makes up part of the Araripe Plateau near the town of Jardin in northeastern Brazil. Santana Formation, Romualdo Member. (Value range E).

Figure 02-095. *Rhacolepis* sp. Santana Formation, Romualdo Member, Araripe Plateau, Jardin, Brazil. The insect bearing Crato Formation underlies the Romualdo Member of the Santana Formation.

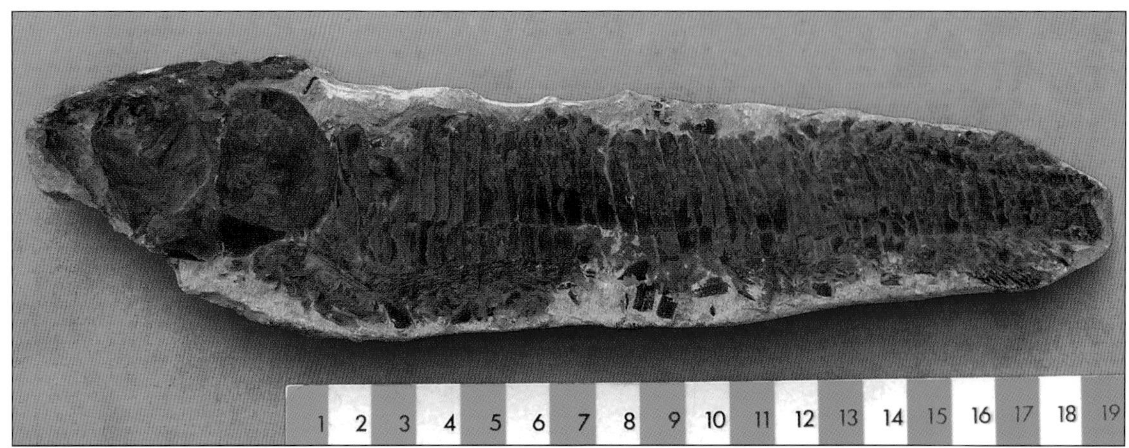

Figure 02-096. *Belonostomus (Vinctifer) comptoni.* A primitive teleost from the Santana Formation of the Araripe Plateau, Jardin, Brazil.

Figure 02-097. *Belonostomus (Vinctifer) comptoni*. Probably the most common of the Santana fish fossils. These are found in concretions that can outline the shape of the body of the fish.

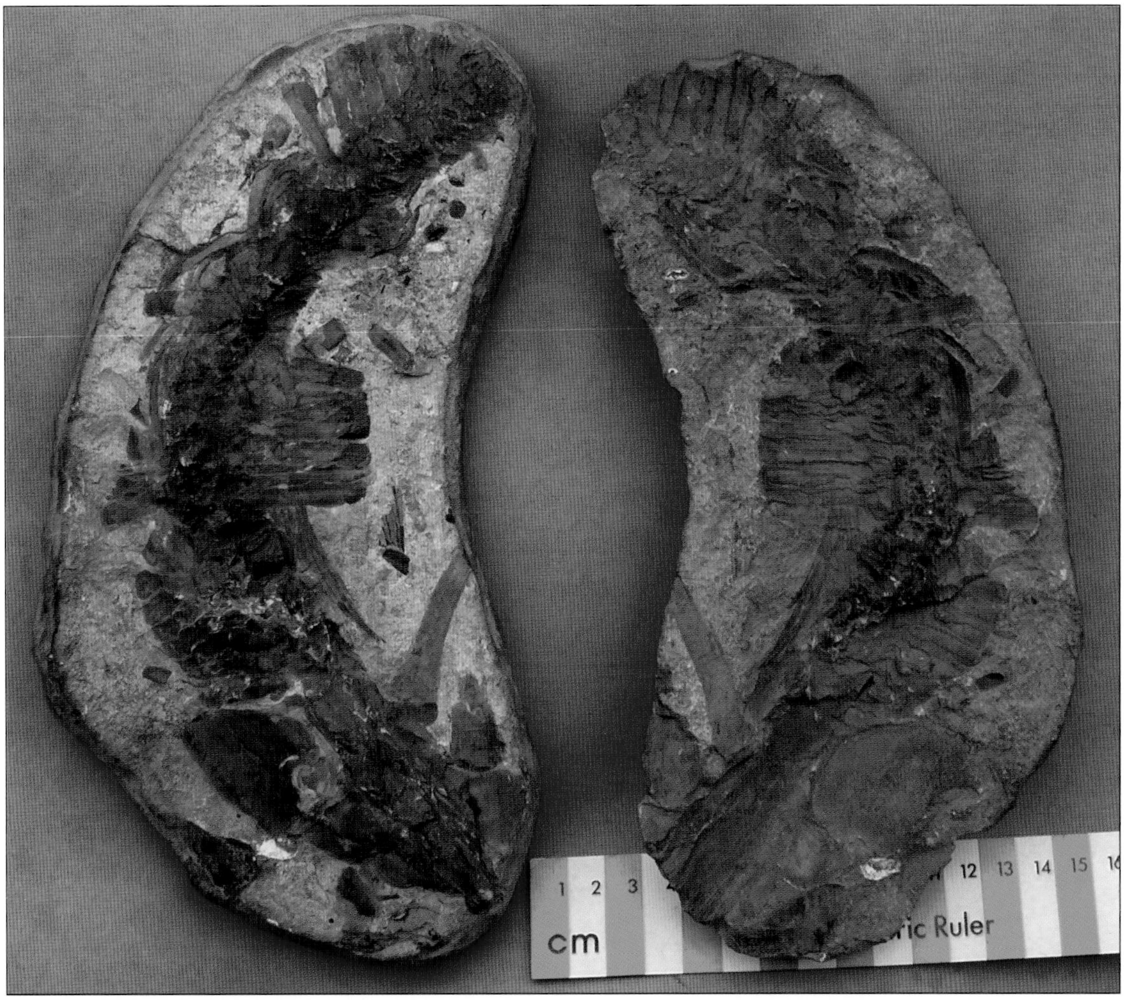

Figure 02-098. *Belonostomus (Vinctifer) comptoni*. A disarticulated specimen of a type available at a low price and which used to be widely seen in the tourist markets of Brazil. *Specimen courtesy of Karoline Stinchcomb*. (Value range F).

Figure 02-099. *Tharrias cirarpis*. Santana Formation, Araripe Plateau, northeast Brazil.

Figure 02-100. *Cearana* sp. This primitive teleost is one of the common fossils of the Santana Formation of northeastern Brazil. This specimen has been hastily prepared for the tourist industry to sell at a low price. Santana fish are incredibly well preserved but to show this feature, the fossil has to be very carefully prepared, a process which can be quite time consuming. (Value range F).

Figure 02-101. *Cearana* sp. A specimen similar to that above but prepared more carefully, hence it has a higher value. Preparation is often a major factor that gives a fossil value. Poorly prepared specimens of the same fossil will be of considerably less value than will be identical ones that are well prepared. *Specimen courtesy of Steven Riggs Jones*. (Value range E).

Figure 02-102. A particularly elongated gar pike from the Santana Formation.

Reptiles

The best known reptiles in the Cretaceous are inosaurs. Lower Cretaceous dinosaurs are known vorldwide, however, not many dinosaur fossils f this age have entered the fossil market, unlike ne situation in the Upper Cretaceous where a fair mount of dinosaur material is available.

Bibliography

Reeside, John B., 1957. "Paleoecology of the Cretaceous seas of the western interior of the United States" **in** *Treatise on Marine Ecology and Paleoecology*, Geological Society of America, Memoir 67.

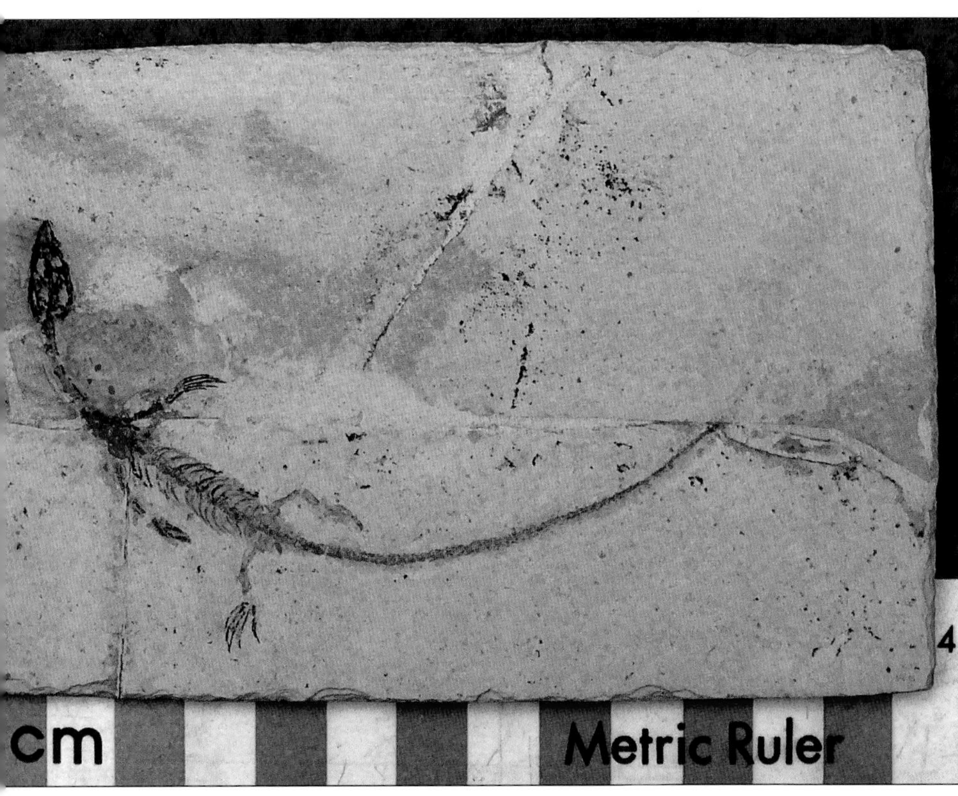

Figure 02-103. *Hyphalosaurus lingyuanensis*. A long-necked, delicate aquatic reptile, one of the spectacular, yet relatively common fossils from Yixian Formation, Jehol, Liaoning, northeast China (Manchuria). The sequence of strata of Liaoning Province spans the Jurassic-Cretaceous boundary and these fossils are often labeled as both late Jurassic or early-most Cretaceous. (Value range E).

Figure 02-104. Raptor claw (cast), possibly from Spinosaurus? Fossil remains of carnivorous dinosaurs can be relatively rare, claws such as this even rarer. This is a cast of the business end of what was most likely a nasty predator like that highlighted in the movie *Jurassic Park*, although this raptor is from the Lower Cretaceous, not the Jurassic. (Value range F).

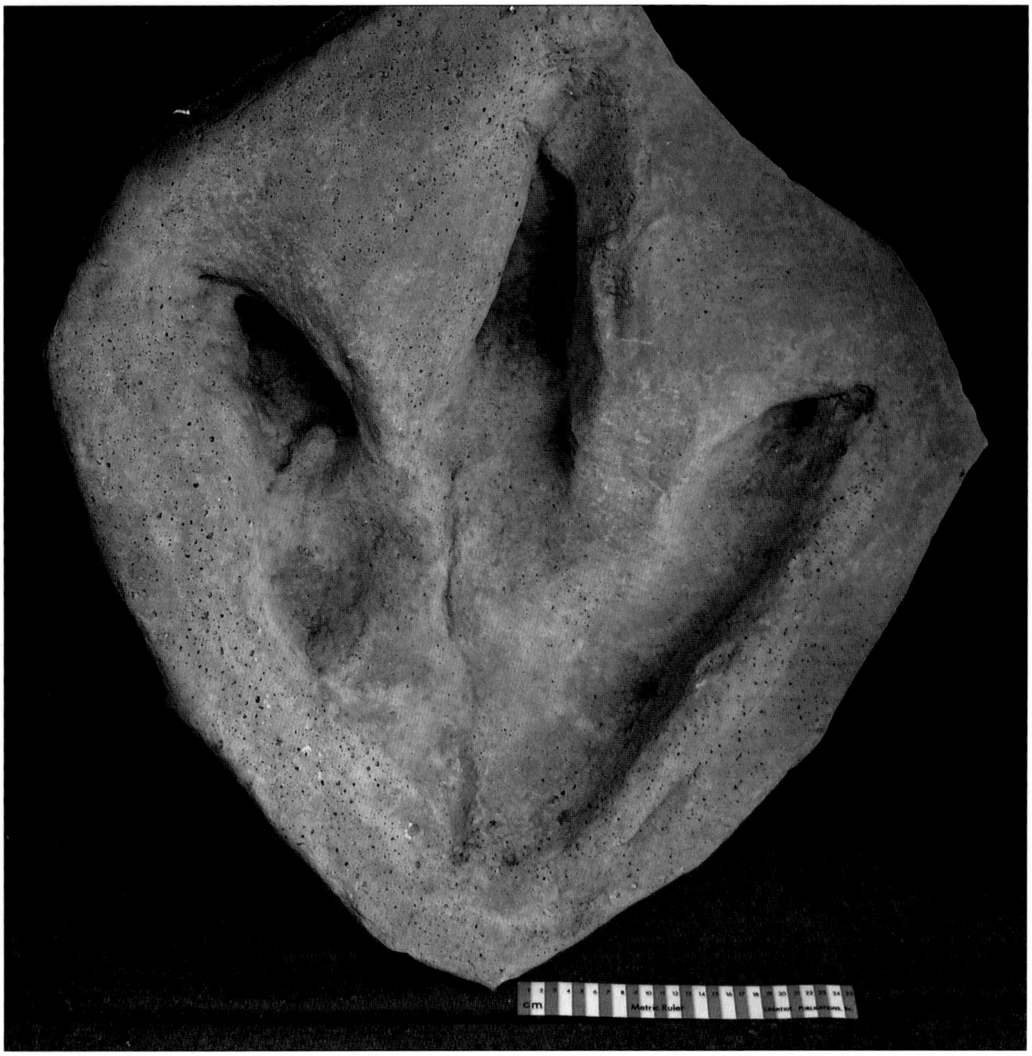

Figure 02-105. Sauropod track. Paluxy River, Texas. Large dinosaur tracks (and related trackways) occur on major bedding planes of the Glen Rose Limestone near Glen Rose, Texas, and elsewhere where the Glen Rose Limestone crops out—which includes southwest Arkansas. These large tacks have aroused interest in dinosaurs for decades after being first discovered in the early 1930s. These come from one of the most extensive occurrences of large dinosaur tracks known—the tracks occurring on major bedding planes of the Glen Rose Limestone; this is a replica made of cement. Casts such as this have been distributed as cement yard ornaments. The Paluxy River trackways are unusual in that they are preserved in a bed of limestone. This has given rise to the suggestion that large sauropods may have ventured out into shallow seaways like that in which the Glen Rose Limestone was deposited, the large dinosaurs being buoyed up by water. (Value range E).

Figure 02-106. *Psittacosaurus* sp. An articulated, early ceratopsian dinosaur. Articulated skeletons of this early type of "horned dinosaur" have been found in quantity in central Asia. This specimen, one of hundreds found is in the Bollinger County Missouri Museum of Natural History, Marble Hill, Missouri.

Chapter Three

Upper Cretaceous-I: Algae through Nautaloids

Stromatolites and Oncolites

These are structures called stromatolites, which were (and are) produced by some of the most primitive photosynthetic life on Earth, the cyanobacteria, known also as blue-green algae. Fossils of cyanobacteria in the form of stromatolites go back as far as 3.5 billion years and evidence for photosynthetic activity to almost **four** billion years.

Figure 03-001. Oncolite formed on an igneous rock "core." This fossil is a "throwback" to two billion years before the Cretaceous; the structure was produced by cyanobacteria (blue green algae) on the surface of an igneous cobble laying in a Cretaceous (?) lake. An oncolite is similar to a stromatolite, differing from a "strom" in that the object on which the "algae" grew periodically moved around like these igneous cobbles did. Such movement allowed the igneous "core" to be covered on all sides by the cyanobacterial (algal) deposits. A number of these interesting "retro" fossils from Mexico have shown up on the fossil market. Lady of Angles Lake near Ascension, Chihuahua, Mexico. (Value range E).

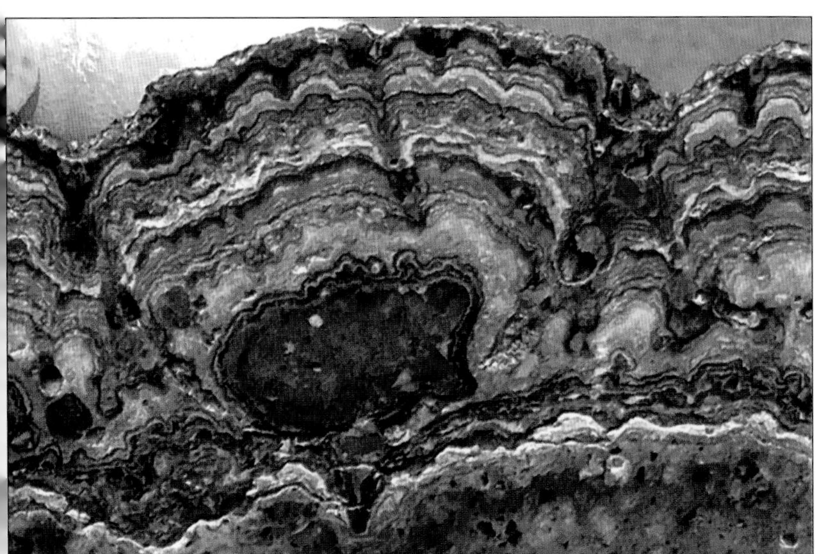

Figure 03-002. Close-up of stromatolite on a small pebble associated with the above specimen. Ascension, Chihuahua, Mexico.

Plants

Ferns and tree ferns were potential food for herbivorous dinosaurs.

Figure 03-003. Fern. Ferns of the family Osmundia were an important element of Late Mesozoic vegetation and were as abundant in its subtropical environment then as they are today. Such fossil ferns are often associated with the vegetation of angiosperms. Frontier Sandstone (?), Rattlesnake Range west of Casper, Wyoming. (Value range G).

Figure 03-004. Osmundaceous fern, Upper Cretaceous, Rattlesnake Range, Wyoming.

Figure 03-005. One of the ferns favored by herbivorous dinosaurs of the late Cretaceous (?) Lance Formation, New Castle, Wyoming. (Value range F).

Conifers were widespread plants which, like *Taxodium* and *Metasequoia*, lived in swamps for thousands of years, eventually accumulating sufficient plant material to form thick beds of coal.

Figure 03-006. *Metasequoia* sp. A variety of primitive conifers such as Cypress, Sequoia, and Metasequoia were common plants in the Late Cretaceous but these primitive conifers can be difficult to distinguish from each other. They can be common fossils not only in the Late Cretaceous but occur well into the Cenozoic Era where they sometimes accumulated in vast quantities to form coal beds. Upper Cretaceous, Lysite, Wyoming. (Value range G).

Figure 03-007. Outcrop of tilted coal beds composed primarily of what originally were massive amounts of primitive conifers such as **metasequoia** and *taxodium*. Little Tonzona River, near Fairwell, Alaska.

Figure 03-008. Close-up of the previously shown coal bed, which originally was composed of primitive conifers. Extensive and thick coal seams mined in eastern Wyoming such as that mined around Gillette, Wyoming, as well as in southeastern Montana, are similar in their "botanical" make-up to this outcrop in Alaska. Coal beds themselves, however, are generally poor sources of quality fossils. The coal chunk in the middle contains blebs of poor quality fossil resin (amber) derived from the conifers.

Figure 03-009. Closer look at the same coal chunk showing small amber "blebs." Rarely is this coal associated "amber" of any quality, as pieces are small, highly fractured, and crumbly. Cretaceous amber of quality is known from New Jersey, Tennessee, Manitoba, and the north slope of Alaska. At all of these locations, fossil insect inclusions have been found, with the amber of New Jersey having the greatest variety. The latter occurred as the amber-bearing horizon was exposed in the grading for a housing subdivision, which uncovered a large area of Cretaceous amber bearing clay. Cretaceous amber generally occurs in smaller pieces than younger amber and insect inclusions are generally rare.

Figure 03-010. Dipping (tilted) coal outcrop along the Little Tonzona River, Alaska. Shown is a yellow, iron carbonate concretion, which formed in the coal seam. Note accompanying field accessories, light meter, rock hammer, and pistol for emergency encounters with bears.

Figure 03-011. Close-up of the above concretion embedded in the somewhat weathered coal layers. Such concretions are sometimes confused with being dinosaur eggs! Being dinosaur eggs would be almost impossible as dinosaurs rarely ventured into the coal swamps. Rock filled, Late Cretaceous dinosaur footprints have, however, been found at the **top** of coal seams in eastern Utah and western Colorado, where they now occur in the roof of the coal mines. These large, sandstone-filled tracks are dangerous to miners for when the coal is removed, the large, heavy sandstone-filled tracks loosen and can fall from the mine's ceiling.

Figure 03-012. Metasequoia leaves with corresponding illustration of the same type of fossil leaves from Charles Lyell's *Elements of Geology*. These came from strata near the Mesozoic-Cenozoic boundary, southeastern Montana. (Value range G).

Figure 03-013. *Glyptostrobus* sp. A leaf spray of a conifer locally common in both the late Mesozoic and early Cenozoic. Rattlesnake Range, Wyoming. (Value range G).

Figure 03-014. *Glyptostrobus* sp. A cluster of conifer twigs from the Rattlesnake Range, Wyoming. These have been confused with tuffs of fossil mosses, which they resemble. (Value range G).

Flowering plants or angiosperms become abundant in the Upper Cretaceous for the first time. The appearance of angiosperms was a monumental event in the history of life as seeds, nuts, and fruit of these plants are high in energy (they contain high energy lipids and carbohydrates) and could be used as a food source for high-energy-requiring animals like mammals and birds.

Figure 03-017. *Banksia* sp. The end of these "willow-like" leaves have a drip tip, a characteristic of tropical trees living in a wet, rainforest-like climate. McNairy Formation, Commerce, Missouri. (Value range F).

Figure 03-015. *Banksia* sp. A willow-like angiosperm from sediments deposited at the head of the Gulf of Mexico when it was as far north as Missouri and Illinois. This is a common Late Cretaceous angiosperm, which resembles but was probably not a true willow. It probably represents a type of **extinct** angiosperm, which only resembles the leaf of a willow. If it was a willow, fossil pollen of willow should be expected to be found in this shale or in rocks of the same age elsewhere and it is not. McNairy Formation, Commerce, Missouri, Crowley's Ridge. (Value range G).

Figure 03-018. *Ficus* sp. The fig tree is an early angiosperm, which can occur locally in the late Cretaceous. This fig leaf compression came from a paleokarst filling associated with a geologically complex, faulted area in southeastern Missouri near Marble Hill. The Marble Hill fault complex has associated with it the Missouri Dinosaur site (See Chapter Six). (Value range F for similar specimens).

Figure 03-016. *Banksia* sp. Leaves of a willow-like angiosperm. Such leaves are suspect as to being true willows as fossil willow pollen is unknown until much later in the geologic record. McNairy Formation, Commerce, Missouri.

Figure 03-019. *Ficus* sp. These internal molds of fossil figs occur in ferruginous (iron rich) sandstone. They can be locally abundant in sandstones of Upper Cretaceous age and a number of them have been acquired by and distributed through collectors over the years. Figs were a probably food source for late Mesozoic hadrosaurs (duckbill dinosaurs) as fragments of their fruit have been identified in what are believed to be hadrosaur coprolites. Herbivorous dinosaurs became particularly abundant during the late Cretaceous when flowering and fruiting plants became a dominant element of the Earth's vegetation. Hell Creek Formation, Glendive, Montana. (Value range F, single specimen).

Figure 03-021. Fruits and seeds of Mesozoic angiosperms were usually small like these. Such fruit provided food for Late Cretaceous land animals, which included the herbivorous dinosaurs such as duck bills (Hadrosaurs) as well as small, marsupial mammals. Angiosperm fruit and seeds of the Cretaceous, being small, didn't provide the quantity of food value found in later (and modern) fruits and seeds. Herbivorous dinosaurs probably had to consume a lot of them to get sufficient nourishment. Upper Cretaceous (Frontier Formation?), Rattlesnake range, Wyoming.

Figure 03-020. *Magnolia* sp. The magnolia is an early angiosperm whose leaves can be found locally in Upper Cretaceous rocks. This specimen is from a paleokarst filling associated with a complex faulted area near the town of Marble Hill in southeast Missouri. (Value range F for similar specimens).

Figure 03-022. This small leaf of an early angiosperm came from the Laramie Formation of the Front Range of Colorado. These plants lived in what was, in the Late Cretaceous, a tropical rain forest; they are from near Golden Colorado. Mesozoic angiosperms are generally rarer than early Cenozoic ones, which often look similar). (Value range G for similar material).

Figure 03-023. This is a common leaf found in late Cretaceous lignitic beds, which formed at the northernmost part of the Gulf of Mexico at the end of the Cretaceous Period. Ripley Group, Ardeola, Missouri. (Value range F).

Figure 03-024. This elongate leaf has a drip tip, which is an elongate point located at the end of the leaf. Drip tips are characteristic of angiosperms, which live in warm, wet, tropical climates. Montana and much of the rest of North America had such a climate during the Cretaceous. Hell Creek Formation, Great Falls, Montana. (Value range F).

Figure 03-025. *Sabalites sp*. A fossil palm. Palms appear in the late Cretaceous along with other angiosperms. Palms are tropical plants and their presence attests to tropical conditions, which occurred widely during the late Mesozoic. Such a tropical climate extended to high latitudes during the Late Cretaceous. These tropical plants lived before the Rocky Mountains were uplifted, an event which—when the mountains formed, drastically changed the climate of North America. Laramie Formation, Golden, Colorado. (Value range F).

Figure 03-026. Petrified angiosperm wood. Petrified wood of Cretaceous age can be locally common in Cretaceous non-marine strata. Determining the specific type of tree from which the wood represents can be difficult other than determining that they are from an angiosperm. Anything more specific than this requires the making of a thin section and its examination by a person knowledgeable in the subtle differences in microstructure of wood types. Specimen at the right is from late Cretaceous strata of central Wyoming (Rattlesnake Range); two specimens to the left are from Cretaceous sediments on Crowley's Ridge, southeastern Missouri. (Value range G for single chunk).

Figure 03-027. "Fossil house:" A house in San Antonio, Texas, made from petrified angiosperm wood (some of it Upper Cretaceous in age). Petrified wood can locally be abundant in Upper Cretaceous rocks of non-marine origin; such strata occur locally in Texas and in nearby Mexico. Note the white Lower Cretaceous ammonite at the lower left side of the entrance.

Figure 03-028. Eve of "fossil house" in San Antonio, Texas. Large masses of petrified wood from angiosperms of either Late Cretaceous or early Cenozoic age were used in its construction. Note the ammonite fragment at the left (*Oxytrophoceras*) and also to the right of the ammonite, a late Paleozoic scale tree root *Stigmaria*. Note another stigmaria fossil to the right of the ventilation opening.

Sponges

The most primitive "animals" of the Cretaceous eas.

igure 03-029. Hexactinellid sponge in flint. The chalk cliffs f southern England (such as form the white cliffs of Dover) ontain flint or chalcedony nodules, some f which, like these, can contain beautiful etrified sponges. (Value range E).

Figure 03-031. Another peek at fossil hexactinellid sponges preserved in flint nodules from "the chalk" along with a woodcut of a sponge from Lyell's *Elements of Geology*.

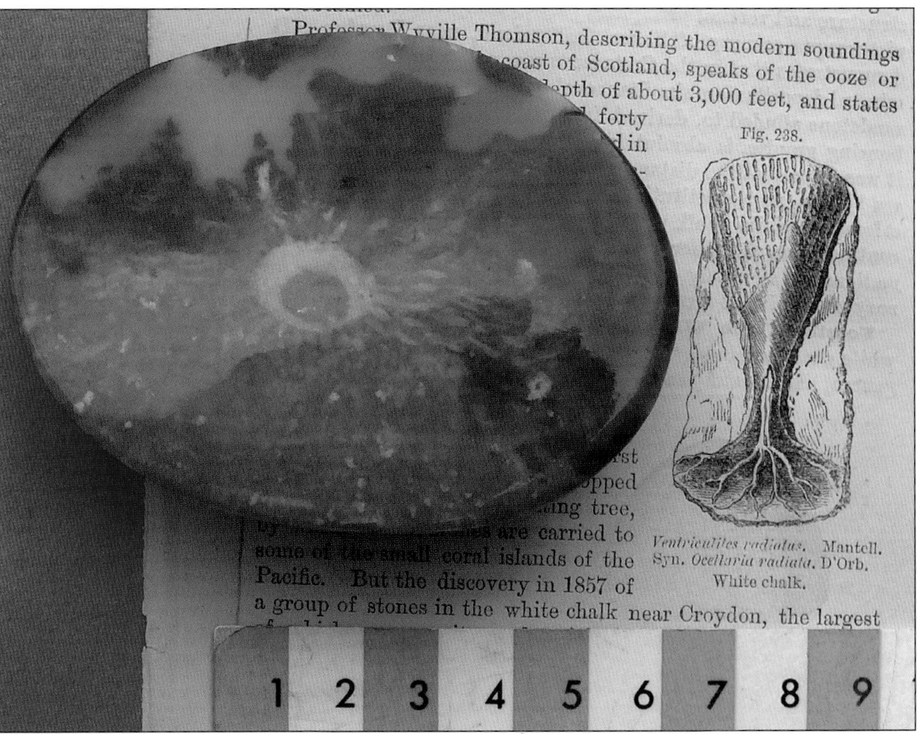

Figure 03-030. Illustration from Charles Lyell's *Elements of Geology* showing a fossil sponge from Cretaceous flints of southern England and a cross section of a fossil sponge in a flint nodule "from the chalk." Sponge fossils in these photos are cross sections of vase-like sponges.

Corals

Not as primitive an animal as a sponge, but corals are still a primitive life form.

Figure 03-032. Colonial coral. Corals are generally rare in Cretaceous rocks for some unknown reason. This is a small colonial coral from the Coon Creek formation, Coon Creek fossil preserve, western Tennessee. (Value range F, rare for the Cretaceous but otherwise corals are common fossils).

Echinoderms

Crinoids in the Upper Cretaceous are relatively rare fossils; these free swimming crinoids are an exception, but they are found in limited areas of the Niobara Chalk of Kansas and Colorado.

Figure 03-033. *Unitacrinus socialis.* A free-swimming crinoid of which large colonies have been found in the Niobara Chal of western Kansas and Colorado. These crinoids floated as rafts in the inland sea, which extended from Texas northwarc to the Arctic Ocean, the North American "Mediterranean." Such crinoids came to be buried in the chalk beds of westerr Kansas, Trego County, Kansas, from where they are best known. *Courtesy of Frank Winter*. (Value range F).

Figure 03-034. *Unitacrinus socialis*. Four specimens of this free-floating crinoid from the Niobara Chalk, Trego County, western Kansas. (Value range F, single specimen).

Figure 03-035. *Unitacrinus socialis*. Part of a large, mounted slab of these free-floating crinoids from the Smoky Hills Chalk of western Kansas. This slab is displayed in the Sternberg Museum in Hays, Kansas, which focuses on Upper Cretaceous fossils found in the chalk beds of the Niobara Chalk of wester Kansas.

Echinoids are the most abundant echinoderms of the Cretaceous. Below is a variety of Cretaceous "urchins" from various parts of the world.

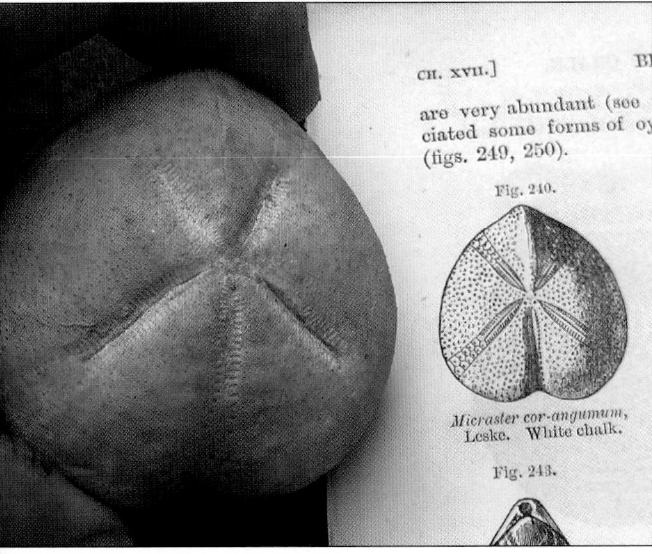

Figure 03-036. *Marsuphites* (*Micraster*) sp. An irregular echinoid from the English chalk. The illustration next to the specimen is also from "the chalk" and is from Lyell's *Elements of Geology*. (Value range F).

Figure 03-037. *Linthia variabilis* Slocom. This group of fossils represents internal molds of thin shelled, small irregular echinoids. They all came from a cluster found in sediments deposited at the northernmost part of the Gulf of Mexico at a time when the Gulf extended into Missouri and Illinois. Crowley's Ridge, Owl Creek Formation, McNairy Group, Ardeola, Missouri. (Value range E for group).

Figure 03-038. *Linthia variabilis* Slocom. Another cluster of small, irregular echinoids (internal molds or steinkerns), which came from Late Cretaceous rocks of Crowley's Ridge, southeastern Missouri. (Value range G for single specimen).

Figure 03-039. *Linthia variabilis* Slocom. Specimens shown here are the same as those shown previously but they were collected from beds deposited just above those of the late Cretaceous in a horizon which some geologists believe represents a tsunami deposit. Such a deposit was formed when an asteroid hit the Earth in the Yucatan region of what is now Mexico. This event is believed to have been **the event** responsible for the Mesozoic extinctions. A tsunami, formed as a consequence of this impact and the massive amount of energy involved was focused and concentrated as it traveled northward, through the Gulf Embayment. As it moved northward, it transported shells and other future fossils, forming concentrations of them at a K/T boundary zone from which these echinoids came. The beds which carried this Cretaceous echinoid are officially Paleocene (early-most Cenozoic in age) but contain Mesozoic fossils like these echinoids as well as the Cretaceous coiled oyster (*Exogyra* sp.). Midway Formation, Olyphant (Possum Grape), Arkansas.

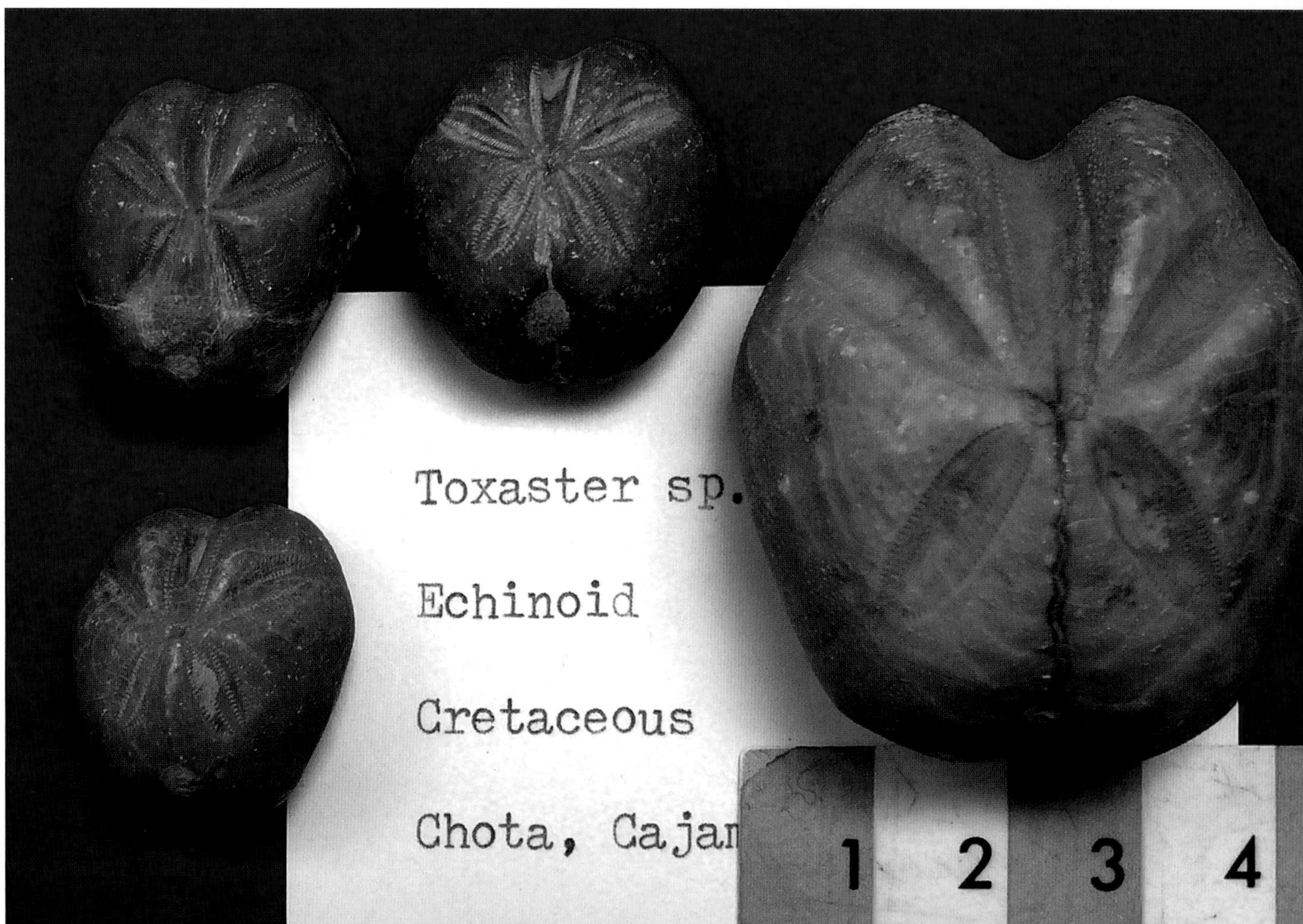

Figure 03-040. *Toxaster* sp. An irregular echinoid similar to those of the previous photos but from Upper Cretaceous rocks of the southern hemisphere. Chota, Cajant, Peru. (Value range F, single specimen).

Figure 03-041. *Hemipreneustus radiatus*. This large irregular echinoid has been collected extensively from chalk beds near Maastricht, Holland, for 200 years. This was one of the fossils that delineated the Cretaceous Period when the geologic time scale was being worked out in the mid-nineteenth century. *Hemipreneustus* is characteristic of the latest Cretaceous, the Maastrichtian, named for Maastricht, Holland. (Value range F).

Figure 03-042. *Echinocorys scutata*. A fairly large irregular echinoid from Cretaceous chalk beds of northern Europe. Dalbyover, Denmark. (Value range F).

Mollusks-Gastropods

Gastropods can locally be abundant fossils in marine Cretaceous rocks. The genus *Turritella* is particularly characteristic.

Figure 03-043. *Volutomorpha gigantea* Wade. These large gastropods come from the famous Coon Creek locality southeast of Memphis, Tennessee. (Value range F).

Figure 03-045. *Volutoderma appressa* Wade. This high-spire gastropod came from the Coon Creek locality, which is now fossil preserve. (Value range E).

Figure 03-046. This is the impression of the "end" of a puzzling fossil which is possibly a scaphopod. It is **not** a gastropod. Owl Creek Formation, Ardeola, Missouri.

Figure 03-044. A group of gastropods from a prolific fossil locality in Tennessee known as the Coon Creek locality. This group of specimens was collected in the 1950s by the author. The elongate gastropods at the left are various species of *Turritella* sp. All of these specimens are from the Coon Creek Formation, Coon Creek, Tennessee.

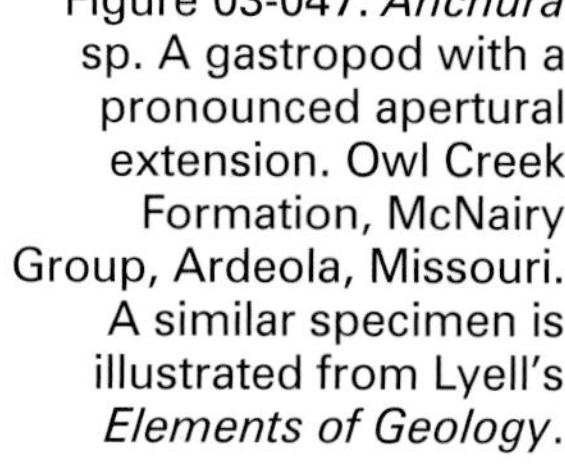

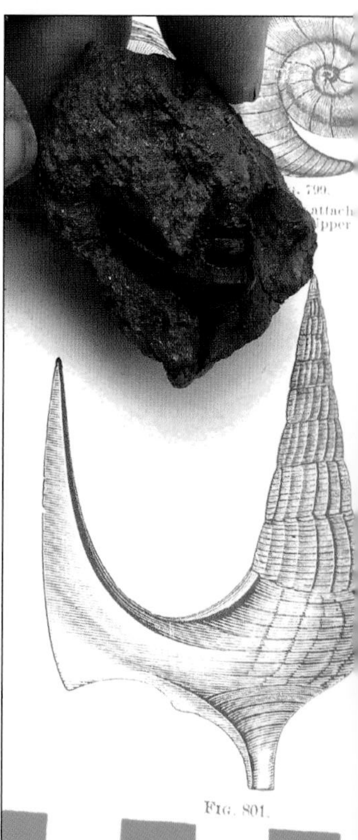

Figure 03-047. *Anchura* sp. A gastropod with a pronounced apertural extension. Owl Creek Formation, McNairy Group, Ardeola, Missouri. A similar specimen is illustrated from Lyell's *Elements of Geology*.

Figure 03-048. A peculiar gastropod similar to that of the previous photo with its long shell extensions. Such gastropods are rare in the Cretaceous; however, Late Cretaceous strata of the Gulf embayment yield an extensive fauna of sometimes-peculiar mollusks like this one. This fossil is an impression and internal mold. Owl Creek Formation, Ardeola, Missouri. (Value range F, rare).

Figure 03-049. *Turritella* cf. *T.mortoni.* Specimens of the gastropod genus *Turritella* are common at the K/T boundary of the Gulf Series in the U.S. The genus *Turritella* has been split into a number of species from the original species *T. mortoni* to define biostratigraphic zones, which occur just above and below the K/T boundary. These specimens are from the Coon Creek (left) and Owl Creek (right) localities. (Value range G, single specimen).

Figure 03-050. *Turritella* cf. *T. vertebroides* Morton. Internal molds and shell replacements of this genus are characteristic of Gulfian sediments. These come from a zone some five feet below the K/T boundary but are the same as those found at the boundary in figures 03-052 to 03-054. Owl Creek Formation, Ardeola, Missouri. (Value range G, single specimen).

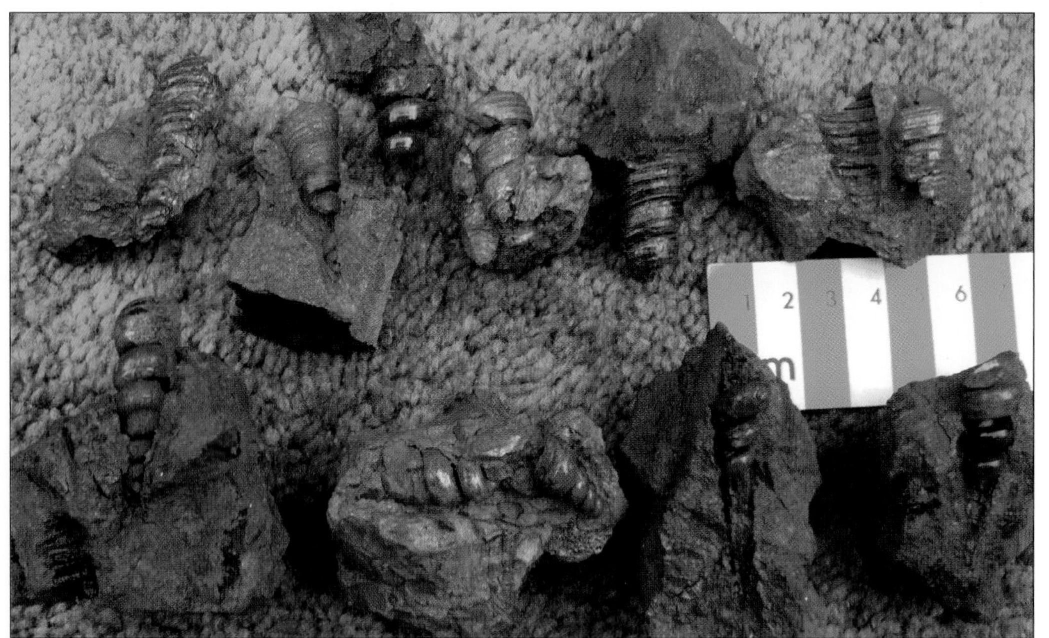

Figure 03-051. *Turritella* sp. A group of internal and external molds of this high spired gastropod particularly characteristic of Gulfian, Late Cretaceous strata. The specimen at the bottom left is the same one as can be seen in outcrops of the Owl Creek Formation shown in Chapter Five. (Value range F for group).

Figure 03-052. *Turritella* cf. *T. mortoni*. These are the internal molds of *Turritella* from a horizon just above the K/T boundary in central Arkansas. A horizon full of these gastropods occurs at the base of the Midway Limestone, a formation normally considered Paleocene in age but which can contain (in its lowermost zones) Cretaceous fossils such as *Exogyra* sp. Some geologists believe that these concentrations of fossils found near the northern (upper) part of the Gulf embayment represent a tsunami deposit. Such a concentration of shells were scoured from the sea floor and concentrated by the tsunami generated from the asteroid impact. This impact formed the large Chicxalub impact structure of the Yucatan Peninsula in the southern Gulf Region of Mexico and produced the Tsunami believed responsible for the clustered shells. Midway Limestone (Clayton or Midway Formation), Olyphant (Possum Grape), Arkansas. (Value range E).

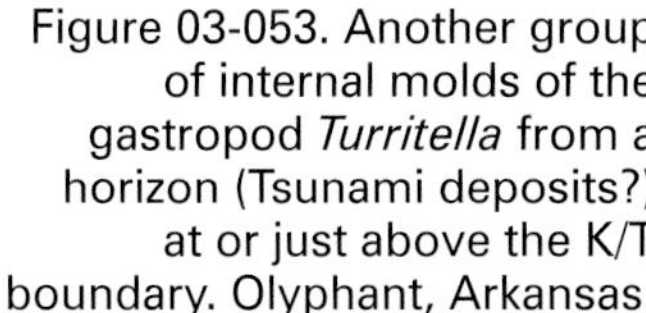

Figure 03-053. Another group of internal molds of the gastropod *Turritella* from a horizon (Tsunami deposits?) at or just above the K/T boundary. Olyphant, Arkansas.

Figure 03-054. Group of *Turritella* cf. *T. mortoni* preserved with some original shell material from at or just above the K/T boundary near Olyphant, Arkansas. *Turritella* and small, distinctive echinoids of the genus *Linthia* sp., both typical of the Upper Cretaceous, are packed together in what may be a tsunami deposit produced from an asteroid impact in the Gulf region of Mexico, (Chicxulub impact structure).

Figure 03-055. *Turritella* cf. *T. mortoni*. These specimens come from a widely dispersed horizon of this gastropod, which occurs just above the K/T boundary. These fossils are from early Paleocene or latest Cretaceous marls which outcrop in King George Co., Virginia in the Chesapeake Bay region.

Mollusks-Pelecypods

Pelecypods are another molluscan class well represented in Upper Cretaceous marine strata. The genus *Inoceramus* is particularly characteristic of the Cretaceous. All representatives of *Inoceramus*, a genus with many species, become extinct at the K/T boundary.

Figure 03-057. *Cucullae vulgaris* Morton. A thick shelled pelecypod locally common in the Upper Cretaceous. With its species name *vulgaris*, I've always wondered what it is that is vulgar about such a nice clam as this? This specimen is from Coon Creek, Tennessee, a site which has produced a wide variety of well-preserved mollusks and is now a paleontological preserve. (Value range G).

Figure 03-056. *Cardium stantuni.* A common pelecypod in the late Cretaceous from Coon Creek, Tennessee.

Figure 03-058. *Inoceramus fragilis* Hall and Meek. A common clam in marine Cretaceous rocks. All species of the genus *Inoceramus* went extinct at the K/T extinction event. Carlyle Formation, Kaycee, Wyoming.

Figure 03-060. *Inoceramus sagensis* Owen. Pierre Shale, Cheyenne River, South Dakota. (Value range F).

Figure 03-061. *Inoceramus sagensis* Owen. Side view of the same specimen as in the previous photo.

Figure 03-059. *Inoceramus simpsoni* Meek. Bearpaw Shale, Forsyth, Montana. (Value range F).

Figure 03-062. *Inoceramus barabina* Morton. Bearpaw Shale, Forsyth, Montana.

Figure 03-063. *Inoceramus simpsoni*. Side view. Nacotah Formation, Arkadelphia, Arkansas. (Value range F).

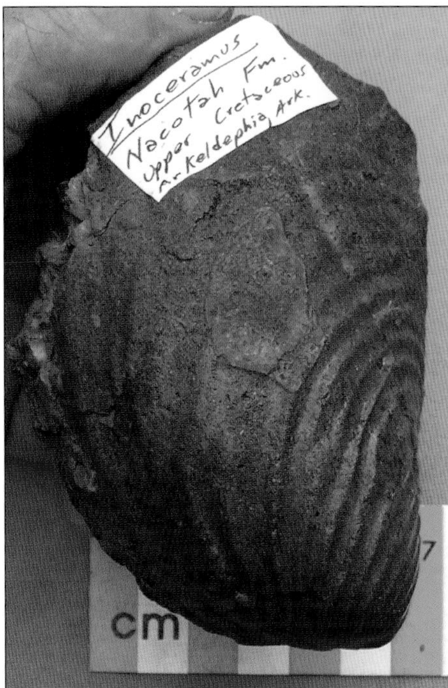

Figure 03-064. *Inoceramus simpsoni*. Front view of same specimen as in figure 03-063.

Figure 03-065. *Inoceramus gilberti*. Chalky limestone deposited in the seaway which split North America into two parts ("North American Mediterranean") can be locally full of this fossil pelecypod but little else. Greenhorn Limestone member of Niobara Chalk, Wilson, Kansas. (Value range G).

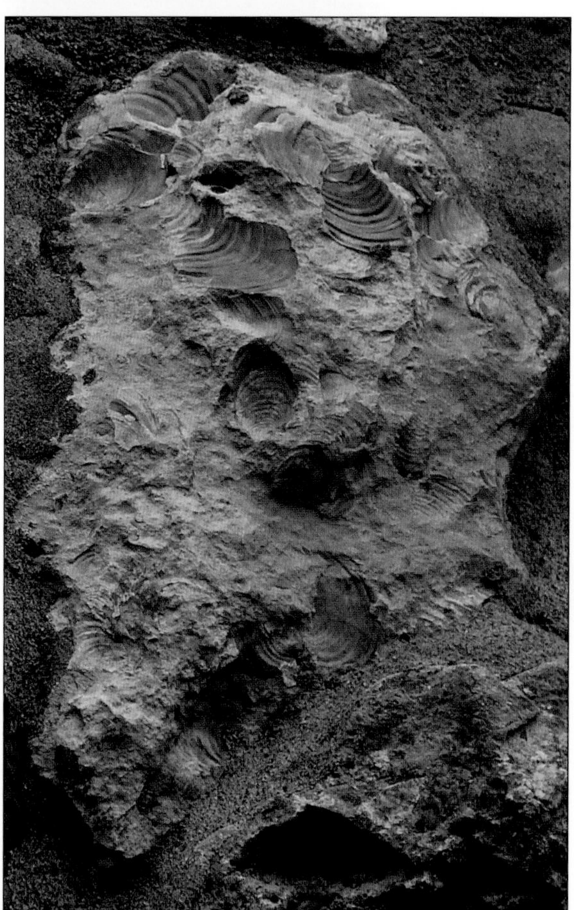

Figure 03-066. *Inoceramus gilberti*. Greenhorn Limestone member of the Niobara chalk. This slab containing specimens of this abundant Cretaceous pelecypod has been set into a rock wall. These pelecypods can be quite abundant in the Greenhorn Limestone, a chalky limestone which occurs at the base of the Niobara Chalk and which crops out abundantly in western Kansas.

Figure 03-067. *Pholadomya tippana* Conrad. Owl Creek Formation, Owl Creek type locality near Ripley, Mississippi. (Value range G, single specimen).

Figure 03-068. *Pholadomya tippana* Conrad. This is a distinctive pelecypod that like *Inoceramus* goes extinct at the K/T boundary. Owl Creek Formation, Ardeola, Missouri. (Value range G, single specimen).

Figure 03-069. *Panope monmouthensis*. A fine clam from the Owl Creek Formation, Ardeola, Missouri. (Value range F).

Figure 03-070. *Trigonia thoracica* Morton. A highly ornamented pelecypod that is rare after the end of the Cretaceous. A species of *Trigonia* still lives in the Indian Ocean of the southern hemisphere. These specimens are from the Coon Creek locality, western Tennessee.

Figure 03-071. Group of mollusks from the Coon Creek locality collected in the 1950s. The elongate fossils are scaphopods. Scaphopods are primitive mollusks that live with elongate shells buried in sediments. Below the scaphopods are specimens of the pelecypod genus *Trigonia*.

Figure 03-072. *Unio* sp. This is a fossil fresh water clamshell (river clam) from river deposits of late Cretaceous age of north central Montana (Hell Creek area). Toward the end of the Cretaceous a series of rivers flowed from west to east, depositing sediments into the seaway to the east; this sea was the so-called North American Mediterranean. Such clams lived in large numbers in these eastward draining rivers. The freshwater deposits from which this clam was collected also contain the bones of large numbers of dinosaurs, including the bones of the famous *T. rex*. Hell Creek Formation, Jordan, Montana.

Figure 03-073. *Pinna* sp. These elongate, mud-burrowing clams are known as razor clams. The genus had its beginning in the mid-Paleozoic and some type of razor clams are still living today. Owl Creek Formation, Owl Creek type locality, near Ripley, Mississippi.

Figure 03-074. *Pinna laqueata*. A straight-shelled razor clam from the Owl Creek Formation. Razor clams represent a long ranging family of pelecypods but they are usually relatively uncommon fossils. Specimens from Crowley's Ridge, Ardeola, Missouri. (Value range F).

Oysters can be very abundant fossils, particularly in Upper Cretaceous chalk where entire oyster banks can be fossilized full of vast quantities of fossil oyster shells. Such common fossils generally have little interest to collectors unless specimens are particularly nice.

Figure 03-075. *Ostrea* sp. These is a type of fossil oyster that can be locally abundant in Late Cretaceous marls of the Gulf Series of the southern states. Specimens shown here are from outcrops along the Chattahoochee River, Columbus, Georgia. (Value range G, single specimen)

Figure 03-076. *Ostrea* sp. Roadside outcrop of chalky marl full of fossil oysters. Such a concentration of oysters represents an example of a fossil oyster bank. Tippah County, Mississippi, c. 1958.

Figure 03-077. *Exogyra costata*. One of the large "coiled oysters" typical of the Upper Cretaceous of the Gulf Series of the southern United States. Tupelo, Mississippi. (Value range G).

Figure 03-078. *Exogyra costata*. This distinctive oyster can be very abundant in Upper Cretaceous marls, which extend from Alabama to Texas. (Value range G).

Figure 03-079. *Exogyra ponderosa*. One of the largest of the "coiled oysters" of Gulf Coast, Upper Cretaceous deposits. (Value range F).

Rudistids are aberrant pelecypods which took on a reef building lifestyle similar to that of corals.

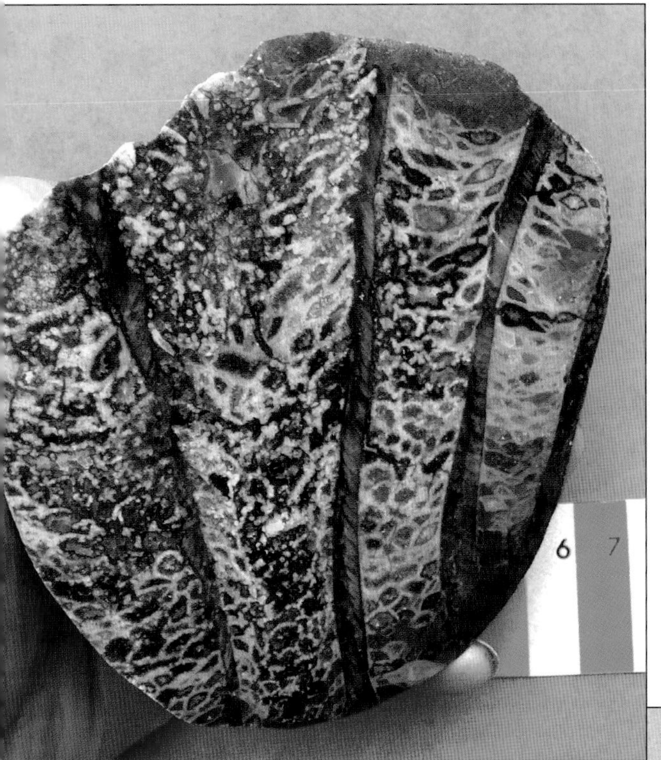

Figure 03-080. *Burnettia* sp. This is a vertical cross section through a rudistid. Rudistids are reef building, aberrant pelecypods found in Cretaceous rocks of the Caribbean region as well as in Texas, Mexico, and central America. These specimens, from Late Cretaceous rocks of Jamaica, were found in marble where Mesozoic rocks, which form the core of this Caribbean Island, were metamorphosed as a consequence of deep burial and later mountain building—as well as being intruded by igneous rocks. The outcrops from which they came are quite hard and resemble the Precambrian rocks that make up much of the basement of North America. In Jamaica, such (Precambrian looking!) rocks form the "basement rocks" of this geologically young island. (Value range F for polished specimen).

Figure 03-081. *Burnettia* sp. A horizontal cross section of a metamorphosed rudistid from Cretaceous rocks of Jamaica. To someone accustom to late Mesozoic rocks being soft and crumbly, this hard rock of the "basement" of Jamaica (and other Caribbean Islands) seems odd–odd in that one would not associate such hard rocks having relatively complex fossils like this in them. (Value range F).

Figure 03-082. *Burnettia* sp. A mineralized, colorful metamorphosed rudistid from Jamaica. Rudistids occupied the ecological niche today occupied typically by corals. *Burnettia* is a mollusk and is **not** a member of the Cnidaria, lower invertebrates that are generally associated with modern reef formers. (Value range F).

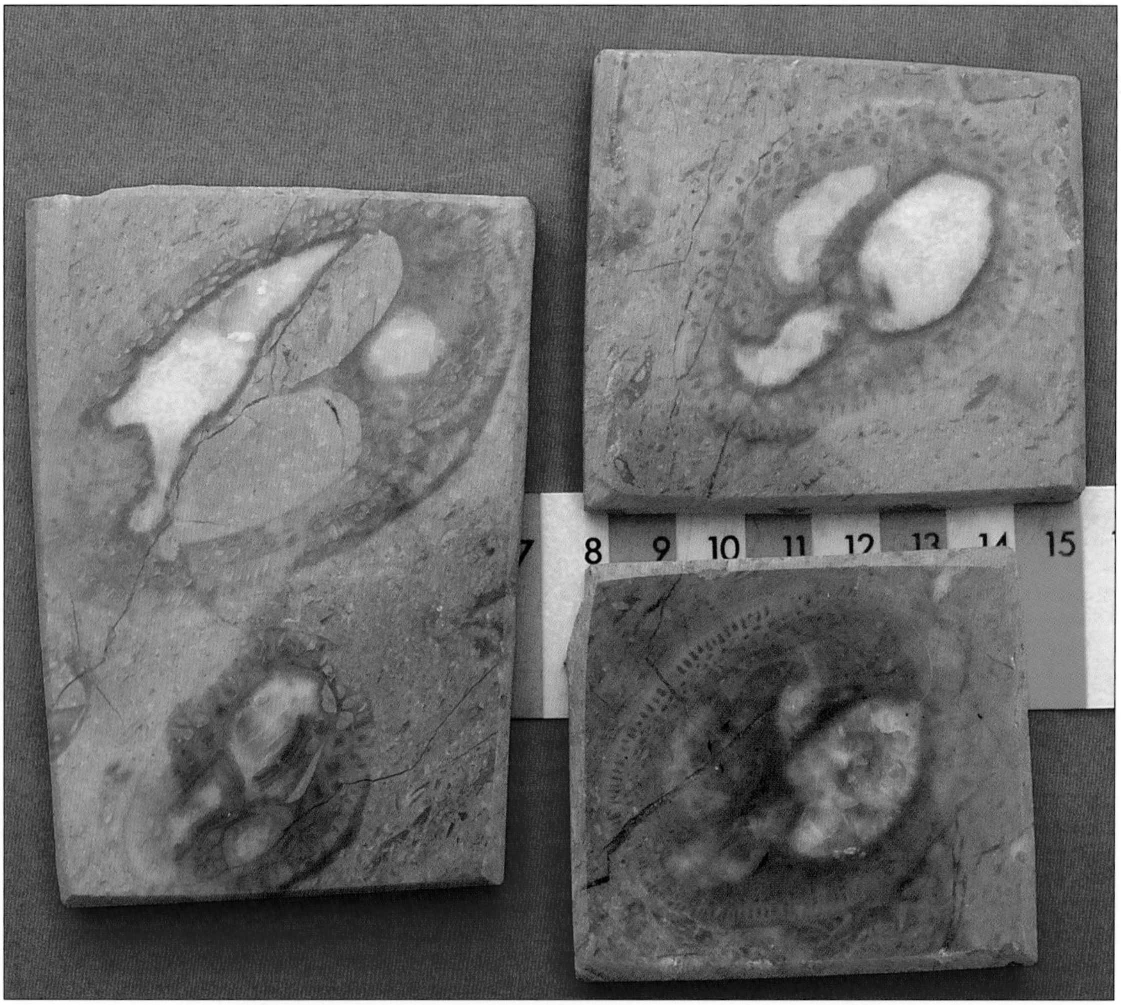

Figure 03-083. Rudistids in hard limestone (marble) from Upper Cretaceous rocks near Monterray, Mexico. Cretaceous limestone is quarried in the vicinity o Monterrey and is cut int marble slabs for floor tiles, which commonly show these fossilized rudistids. Rudistids became the ecological equivalent of corals in the Upper Cretaceous, they are also not found in Cretaceous strata of higher latitudes. (Value range G).

Puzzling or problematic fossils are much less common in Mesozoic rocks than they are in the Paleozoic, particularly the early Paleozoic where the majority of problematic forms occur.

Figure 03-084. *Wapariconus* sp. A problematic (puzzling) fossil from Late Cretaceous rocks of New Zealand. Usually problematic fossils like this are associated with the lower Paleozoic, especially the Cambrian Period. Rarely is a paleontologic puzzle like *Wapariconus* found this late in geologic time. It has been suggested that it represents a type of Rudistid although the structure of *Wapariconus* is different from that of a rudistid, which is a reef forming pelecypod. *Wapariconus* also is not a coral, which it resembles. (Value range E).

Figure 03-085. *Wapariconus* sp. Here is a closeup view of the coral-like structure of this problematic fossil from New Zealand.

Mollusks-Nautaloid Cephalopods

Nautaloid cephalopods represent a large group of shelled mollusks which had a wide range in both diversity and abundance during the geologic past, particularly in the Paleozoic. In the Mesozoic, nautaloids are less diversified. Today, they are represented by only one form, the pearly nautilus.

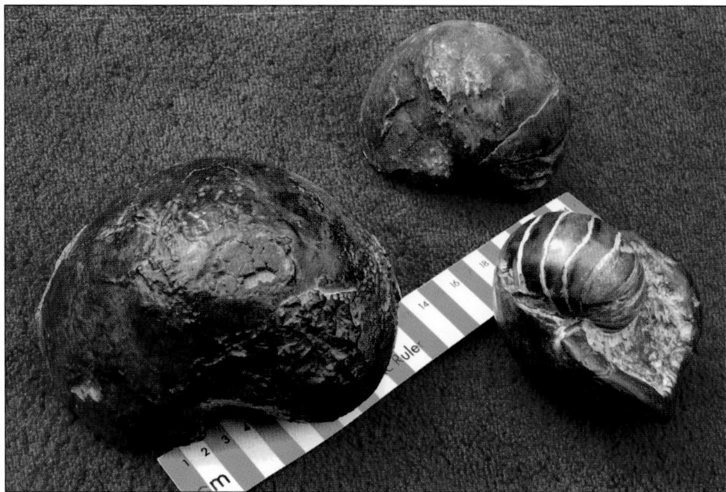

Figure 03-086. *Eutrephoceras* sp. These are coiled nautaloid cephalopods characteristic of the Late Cretaceous. They are similar to the living pearly nautilus which may have descended from *Eutrephoceras. Eutrephoceras* is widespread but is rarely found concentrated in Late Cretaceous marine strata where it occurs with ammonites with which it is associated. The large specimen at the left is from southeastern Missouri (Crowley's Ridge), the specimen to the right is from Saratoga, (southern) Arkansas. The example at the bottom is from the Pierre Shale, Black Hills, South Dakota. (Value range F, single specimen).

Figure 03-087. *Eutrephoceras* sp. The three specimens of this Cretaceous nautaloid are preserved as chalk molds and are from the Saratoga Chalk, Saratoga, Arkansas. (Value range G, single specimen).

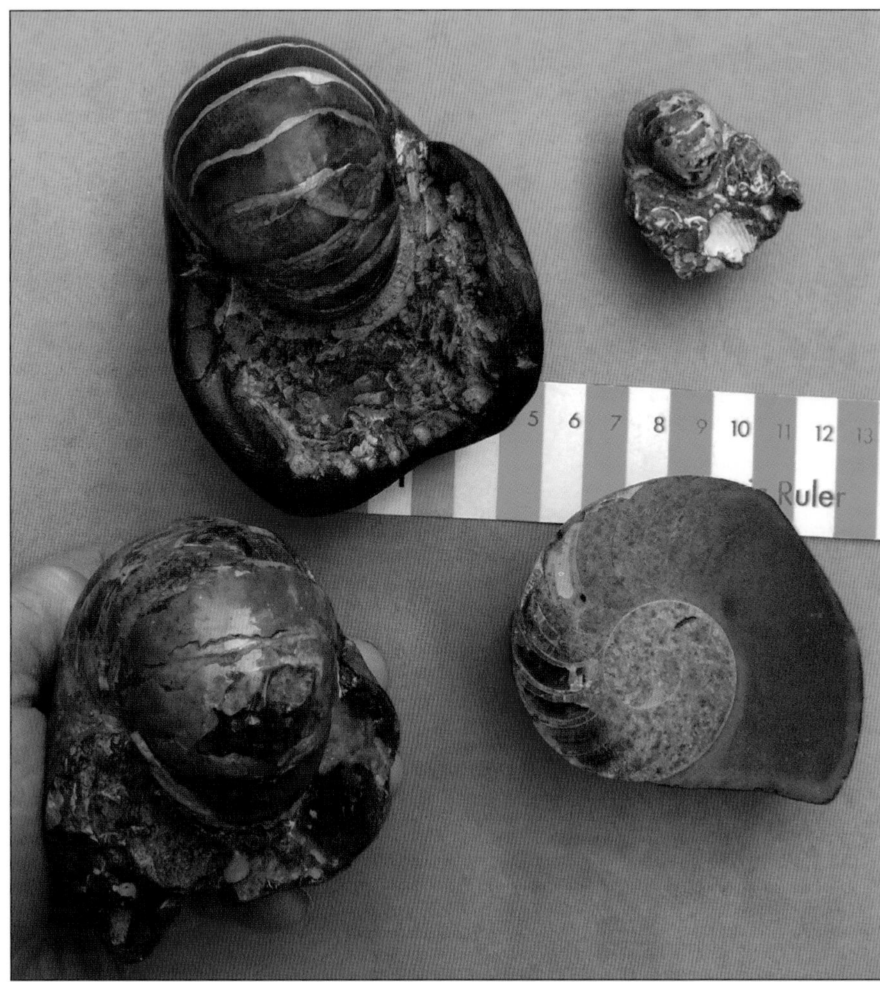

Figure 03-088. *Eutrephoceras dekayi*. Illustrated are three specimens of this distinctive Upper Cretaceous nautaloid from the Pierre Shale near Wasta, South Dakota, and a large specimen from southeast Missouri.

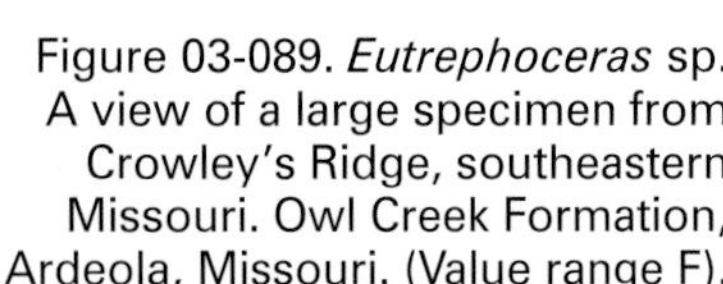
Figure 03-089. *Eutrephoceras* sp. A view of a large specimen from Crowley's Ridge, southeastern Missouri. Owl Creek Formation, Ardeola, Missouri. (Value range F).

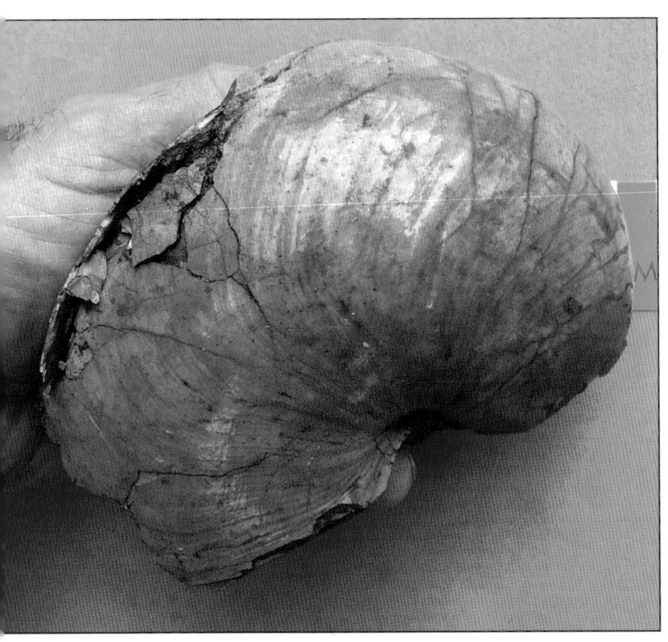

Figure 03-090. *Eutrephoceras* sp. A crushed specimen of this nautaloid preserved with its original shell material. Specimen from Coon Creek, western Tennessee. (Value range F).

Figure 03-091. *Eutrephoceras* sp. Polished specimens of this widespread nautaloid from Madagascar. It occurs associated with ammonites and large numbers of these attractive fossils have entered the fossil market. They are sometimes sold as ammonites—which they are **not**! *Eutrephoceras* (also known with Madagascar specimens as *Cyamatoceras*) generally is found in rocks of Upper Cretaceous age but *Eutrephoceras* is a wide-ranging genus. (Value range F, single specimen).

Figure 03-092. "Kitty litter fossils" Absorbent clay (Fuller's Earth) of early Cenozoic age is mined on Crowley's Ridge in southeastern Missouri. At one of the open pit mines, digging into underlying strata for instillation of a sump pump, numerous Cretaceous molluscan fossils were encountered like those shown here. The concentration of fossils found is believed to be part of a tsunami deposit associated with an asteroid impart in the Gulf of Mexico. At the left are tail vertebrae of a mosasaur found with the molluscan fossils. *Courtesy of Rick Poropat.*

Figure 03-093. Group of fossil mollusks from the kitty litter site containing what are believed to be altered (turned to greenish clay) glass spheres (microtectites) associated with the impact and its massive tsunami.

Chapter Four

Ammonites through Turtles

Ammonites

Probably no other animal (other than the dinosaur) is so strongly associated with the Mesozoic Era as is the ammonite. A shelled cephalopod, ammonites are believed to have had a body similar to that of an octopus—a mollusk that challenges many vertebrates in the complexity of its nervous system. Ammonites diversified into distinctive types in the Triassic and Jurassic and then diversified again in the Late Cretaceous—the heteromorphs of the late Cretaceous being some of the most ornate and peculiar ones known. Ammonites were one of the jewels of the Mesozoic seas with these last ones becoming extinct with the catastrophic event that ended the Mesozoic Era and the Cretaceous Period.

Figure 04-001. The internal mold of one of the last of the ammonites preserved in sandstone of the Mesa Verde Formation, near Cuba, New Mexico. (Value range F).

Figure 04-002. *Discoscaphites* sp. These ammonites come from some of the youngest marine beds of the Upper Cretaceous and are one of the last ammonites to exist, living right before the terminal Mesozoic extinction event. Fox Hills Formation, Dewey County, South Dakota. (Value range F).

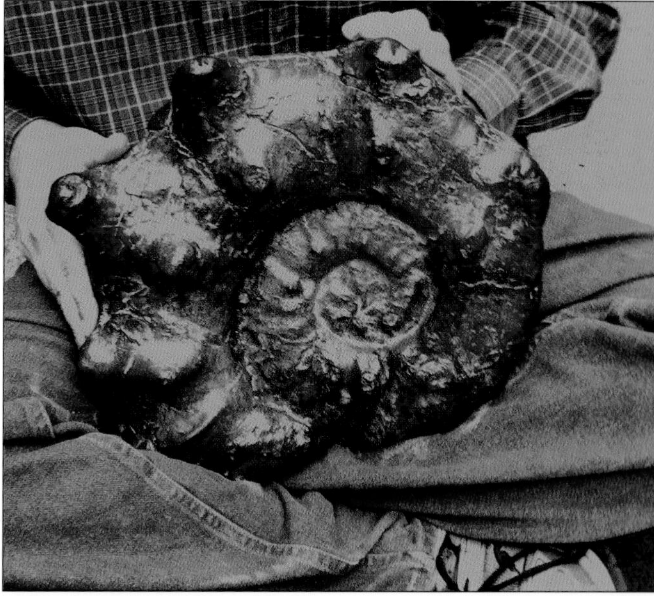

Figure 04-003. This large ammonite was found in the Big Horn Basin in the vicinity of Greybull, Wyoming. Some ammonites found near Greybull have been over four feet in diameter. (Value range E).

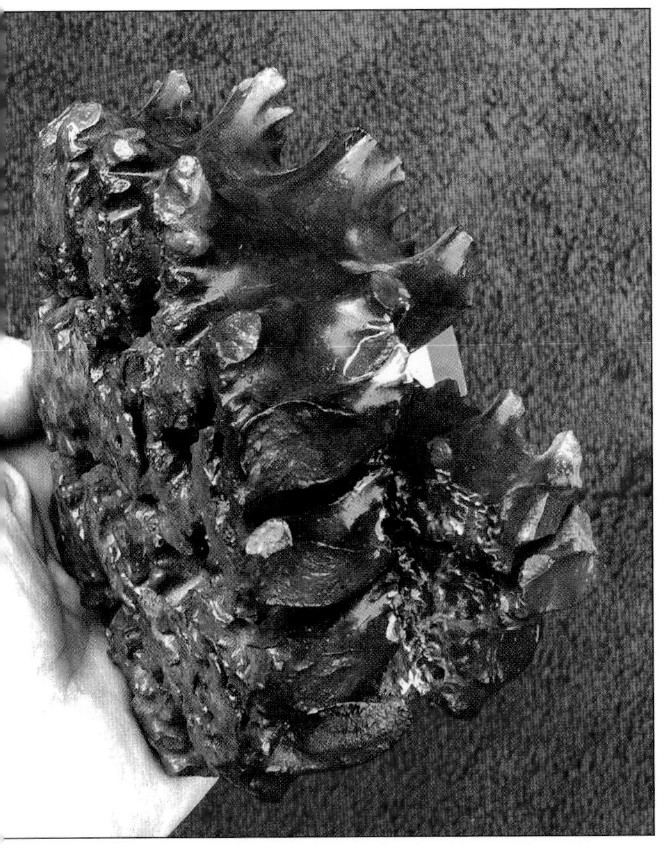

igure 04-004. A portion of one of the large ammonites of he previous photo. Fragments like this chamber filling show omplex ammonite sutures. These can be fairly common ossils in the late Cretaceous of Montana and Wyoming. They esemble a type of puzzle and specimens of these were given eligious significance by the Sioux Indians. (Value range F).

Figure 04-006. *Metoicoceras* sp. Another ammonite cephalopod salvaged by collectors from a cement quarry in the Fort Worth, Texas, area by collectors. Eagle Ford Formation. (Value range E).

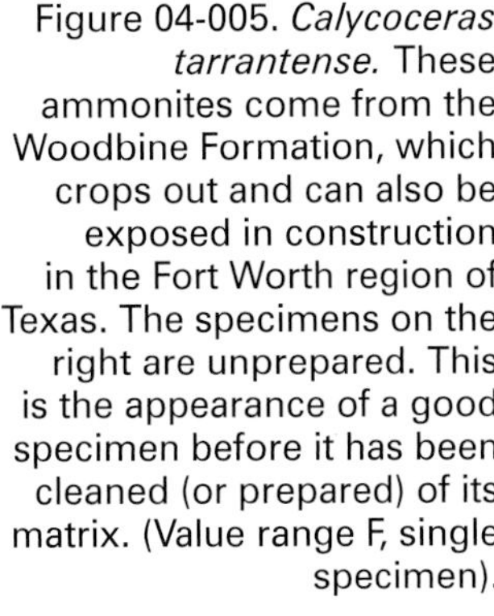

Figure 04-005. *Calycoceras tarrantense.* These ammonites come from the Woodbine Formation, which crops out and can also be exposed in construction in the Fort Worth region of Texas. The specimens on the right are unprepared. This is the appearance of a good specimen before it has been cleaned (or prepared) of its matrix. (Value range F, single specimen).

Figure 04-007. *Scaphites* sp. These ammonites are found in the Dallas-Fort Worth area. Localities for them come and go, most eventually being covered by urbanization. Eagle Ford Formation. (Value range F).

Figure 04-008. *Discoscaphites* sp. A very late Cretaceous ammonite from the Fox Hills Formation of the North American high plains. Edgemont, South Dakota. (Value range F, single specimen).

Figure 04-009. *Sphenodiscus lobatus*. This is one of the last of the ammonites. The genus *Sphenodiscus* has intricate and complex sutures. Here is an internal mold of this ammonite, showing such sutures. *Sphenodiscus* is one of the last ammonites to exist before the K/T extinctions, which occur in strata just above that which produced this ammonite. Walnut Formation, Cleburne, Texas. (Value range E).

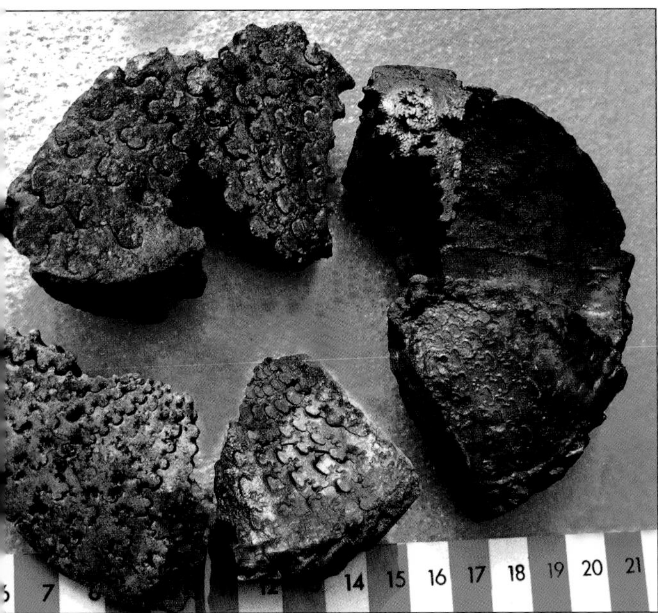

Figure 04-010. *Sphenodiscus lobatus*. This is a fragmented specimen of this latest Cretaceous (Maastrichtian) ammonite from deposits of the Gulf of Mexico when it extended as far north as Missouri. Owl Creek Formation, Ardeola, Missouri.

Figure 04-011. *Engonoceras serpentinum*. This is an internal mold of an ammonite which has become the nucleus of a concretion. Specifically, the ammonite has attracted iron oxide, which has made a partial concretion. Pawpaw Shale, Denton Co., Texas. *Courtesy of John McLeod*. (Value range F).

Heteromorph ammonites: Most ammonites possess streamline-shaped shells, as the animals were presumably excellent swimmers. Some ammonite shells, particularly those of the late Cretaceous exhibit odd shapes, which would seemingly interfere with the animal's ability to swim. Such oddly shaped ammonites are referred to as heteromorphs and range from a mildly irregularly shaped shell like *Scaphites* to twisted or recurved shells which would appear to have impaired most movement of the animal and to have made it almost impossible for it to swim.

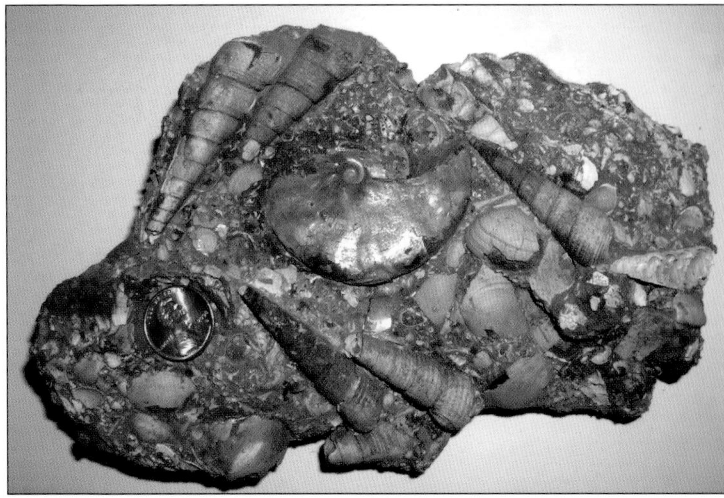

Figure 04-012. *Engonoceras serpentinum*. A concretion containing a specimen of this latest Cretaceous ammonite surrounded by clams and numerous specimens of the gastropod Turritella. Pawpaw Shale, Denton Co., Texas. *Courtesy of John McLeod*. (Value range E).

Figure 04-013. *Scaphites nodosus* Conrad. What is sometimes considered as a type of heteromorph ammonite which came from latest Upper Cretaceous strata of the Gulf Series. These are some of the last of the ammonites occurring just below the K/T boundary when ammonites went extinct. *Scaphites nodosus* somewhat resembles a caterpillar. Owl Creek type locality, Ripley, Mississippi.

Figure 04-014. Another group of *Scaphites nodosus* from the Owl Creek Formation, Owl Creek type locality near Ripley, Mississippi. (Value range E for group).

Figure 04-015. *Scaphites nodosus* Conrad. These are internal molds (steinkerns) of this latest Mesozoic, "bumpy" caterpillar-like ammonite. They occur just below the K/T boundary, Owl Creek Formation, Ardeola, Missouri. (Value range E for group).

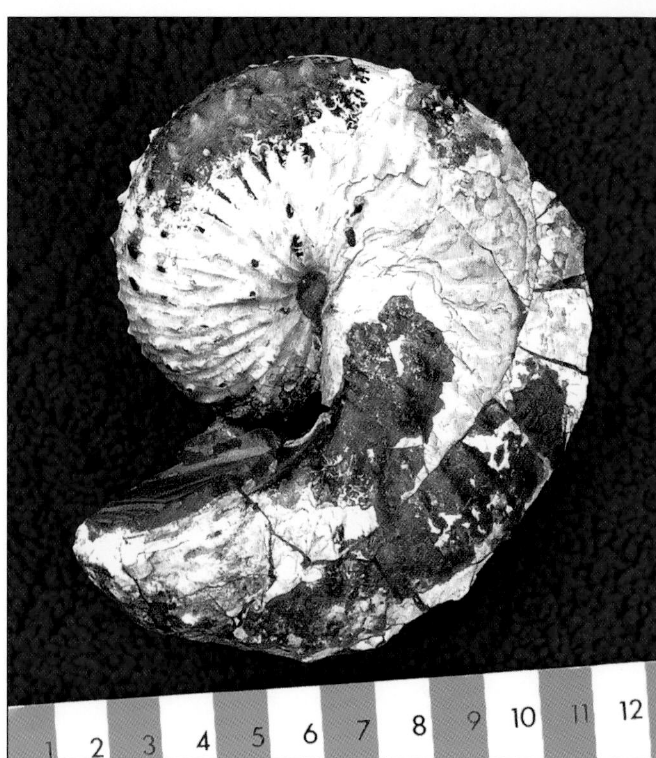

04-016AAA **(*This image is too small at 350 dpi for the AAA sizing. Is a larger version available? Thanks.)**

Figure 04-016. *Acanthoscaphites* sp. This heteromorph ammonite can be locally abundant in the Bearpaw Shale of eastern Montana. (Value range F).

Figure 04-017. *Acanthoscaphites* sp. This specimen is from the Pierre Shale of the Cheyenne River near Wasta, South Dakota. (Value range E).

Figure 04-018. *Hilicoceras* sp. These loosely coiled, heteromorph ammonites are from the Coon Creek Formation of northern Mississippi. Union Co., Mississippi. (Value range F).

Figure 04-019. *Helicoceras navarroense* These loosely coiled ammonites are from the Coon Creek Formation, Tippah County, Mississippi. (Value range F, single specimen).

Figure 04-020. *Helicoceras navarroense*. Specimens of these elongate, high-spired ammonites resemble gastropods. *Didymoceras* has its whorls separated from each other and its outer whorl is disjunct (separated) from the rest. Coon Creek Formation, Union County, Mississippi.

Figure 04-021. *Helicoceras sp.* Loosely coiled heteromorphs. Coon Creek Formation, McNairy Co., Mississippi.

Figure 04-022. *Helicoceras* cf. *navarroense*. A specimen of this heteromorph from the Coon Creek Formation of the Coon Creek fossil preserve, western Tennessee. (Value range E).

Figure 04-023. *Turrilites* sp. The genus Turrilites is a heteromorph ammonite that resembles a high-spired gastropod. Nacotah Formation, Arkadelphia, Arkansas. (Value range F, single specimen).

Figure 04-024. *Nostroceras* sp. A large, single specimen of this heteromorph ammonite from the Coon Creek locality of western Tennessee. (Value range D).

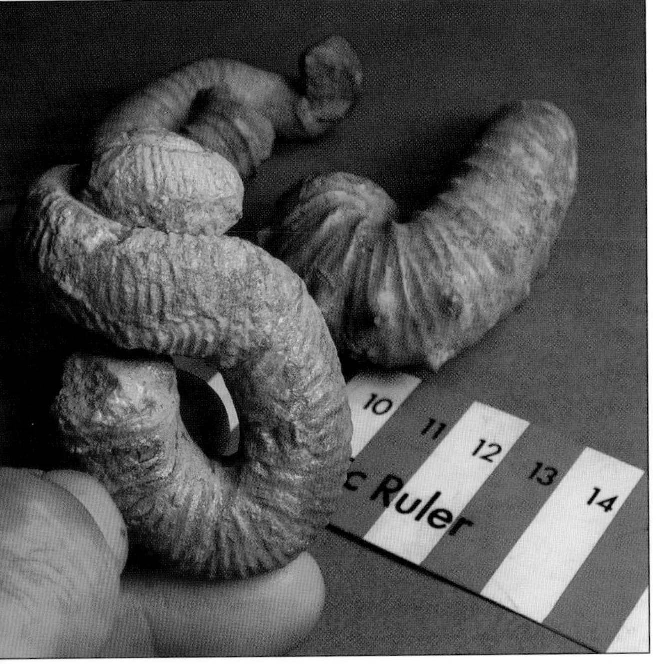

Figure 04-025. *Nostroceras hyatti*. A complete, single specimen of this distinctive heteromorph ammonite. Usually the initial coil of *Nostroceras* is missing and is rarely preserved. Heteromorph ammonites are much sought after and are highly collectable. Saratoga Chalk, Saratoga, Arkansas. (Value range E).

Figure 04-026. *Nostroceras hyatti*. These heteromorph ammonites resemble caterpillars ("catterpiggles"). They can be locally abundant, as were these specimens, which all came from a single limestone boulder excavated in the cuttings of a railroad. Saratoga Chalk, Saratoga, Arkansas. (Value range G, single specimen).

Figure 04-027. *Nostroceras hyatti*. Another group of these distinctive heteromorph ammonites, all are missing the initial coil, a characteristic of most specimens of this species. Saratoga Chalk, Saratoga, Arkansas. (Value range G, single specimen).

Figure 04-028. *Oxybeloceras meekanum*. A particularly aberrant heteromorph ammonite from the Pierre Shale. They are rare and are highly collectable. Wasta, South Dakota. (Value range E).

Figure 04-030. *Didymoceras cheyennense*. Additional spectacular specimens of this heteromorph ammonite from the Pierre shale, Cheyenne River. (Value range C).

Figure 04-029. *Didymoceras cheyennense.* A superb specimen of this heteromorph ammonite from the Pierre Shale, South Dakota. *Courtesy of Steve Holly*. (Value range D).

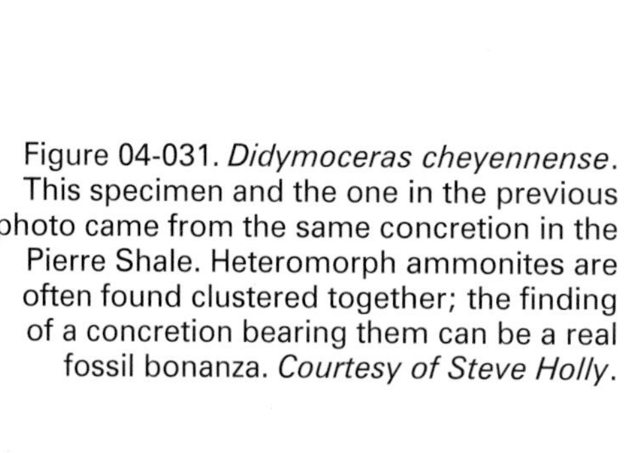

Figure 04-031. *Didymoceras cheyennense*. This specimen and the one in the previous photo came from the same concretion in the Pierre Shale. Heteromorph ammonites are often found clustered together; the finding of a concretion bearing them can be a real fossil bonanza. *Courtesy of Steve Holly*.

Figure 04-032. *Hamulina* sp. This is a genus of heteromorph ammonite that resembles a saxophone. Such an ammonite would presumably have been avoided by a person with "saxophobia." (See Chapter Two). Barremian, Barreme, France. (Value range F).

The genus Baculites is a heteromorph ammonite with a straight or slightly curved shell at the end of which is a small coil which is rarely preserved. *Baculites* is strictly an **Upper Cretaceous** ammonite.

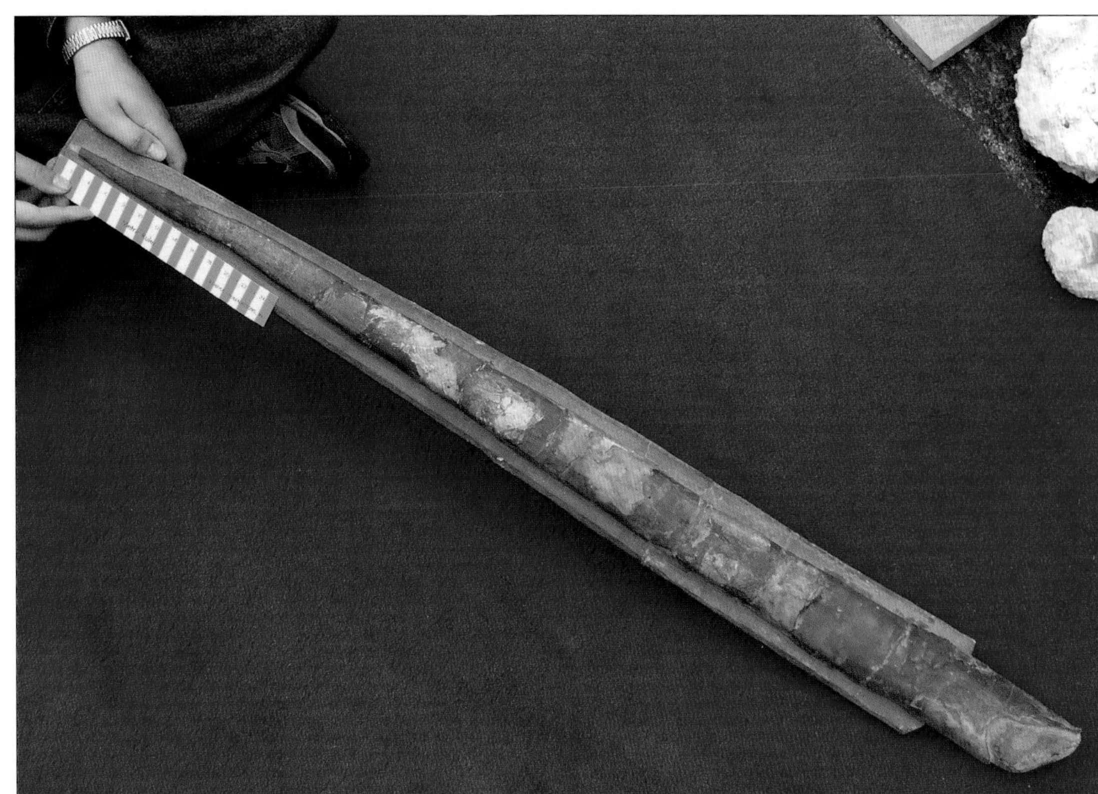

Figure 04-033. *Baculites compressus*. Usually only a part of a Baculites specimen is found preserved in the ironstone concretions of the Pierre Shale. This is a composite specimen showing what the complete animal (sans soft parts) would have looked like. The aperture is preserved on this specimen, a relatively rare occurrence. *Baculites* is a straight heteromorph, occurring widely in Upper Cretaceous sediments of the "North American Mediterranean." Pierre Shale, Wasta, South Dakota. (Value range D).

Figure 04-034. *Baculites ovatus*. Bearpaw Shale, Kaycee, Wyoming.

Figure 04-035. *Baculites compressus*. Section of this straight heteromorph shows the chambers filled with yellow calcite. This is the most common species of *Baculites* in the late Cretaceous of the western U. S., Wasta, South Dakota. (Value range E, for polished specimen).

Figure 04-036. *Baculites ovatus*. A short section of *Baculites* showing its characteristic "mother of pearl" nacre and shell ornamentation. Bearpaw Shale, Forsyth, Montana.

Figure 04-037. *Baculites compressus*. Specimen showing original shell nacre. Pierre Shale, Wasta, South Dakota. (Value range F).

Figure 04-038. This is the same specimen as Figure 04-037, showing the flip side of the ammonite.

igure 04-039. *Baculites compressus*. **Left**: specimen with hell nacre removed showing sutures; **right**: backside of ectioned specimen showing shell chambers with minimal levelopment of sutures in the shell interior. Pierre Shale, Cheyenne River, South Dakota.

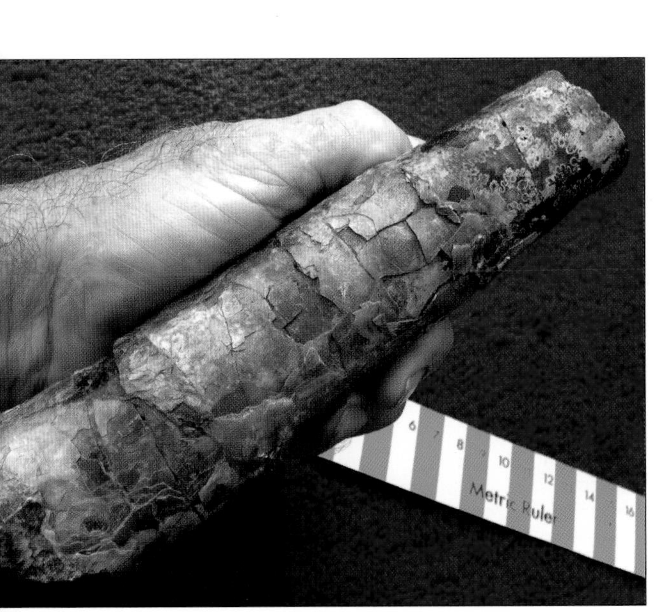

igure 04-040. *Baculites ovatus*. Bearpaw Shale, Kaycee, Wyoming.

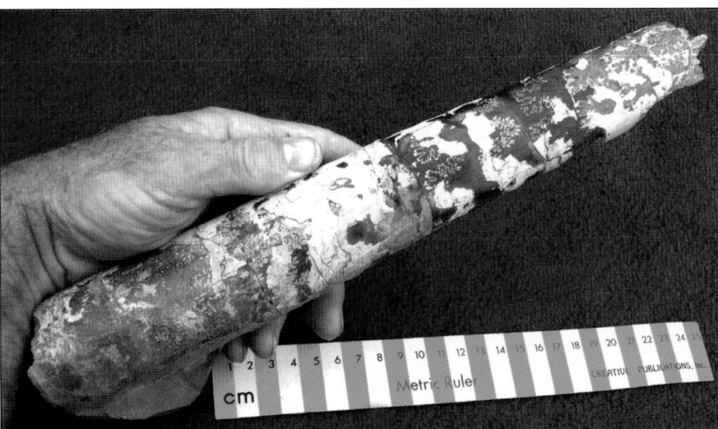

Figure 04-041. *Baculites ovatus*. Pierre Shale, Wasta, South Dakota.

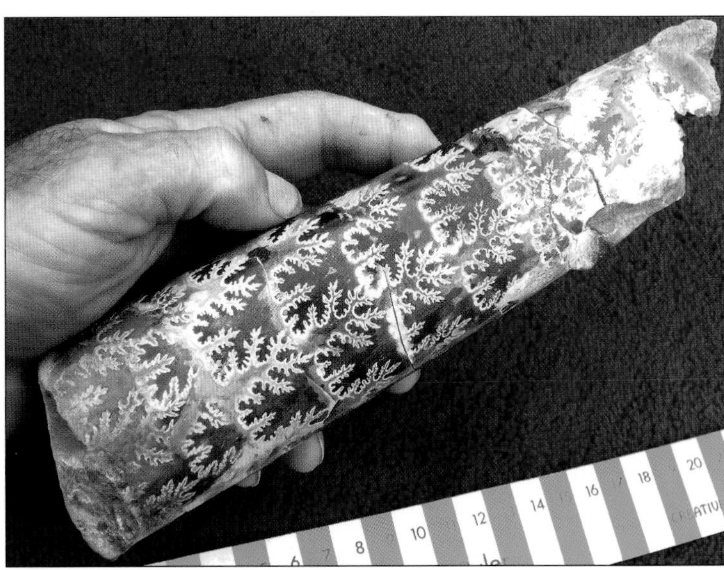

Figure 04-042. *Baculites compressus* with suture pattern nicely shown. Cheyenne River, near Wasta, South Dakota. (Value range E).

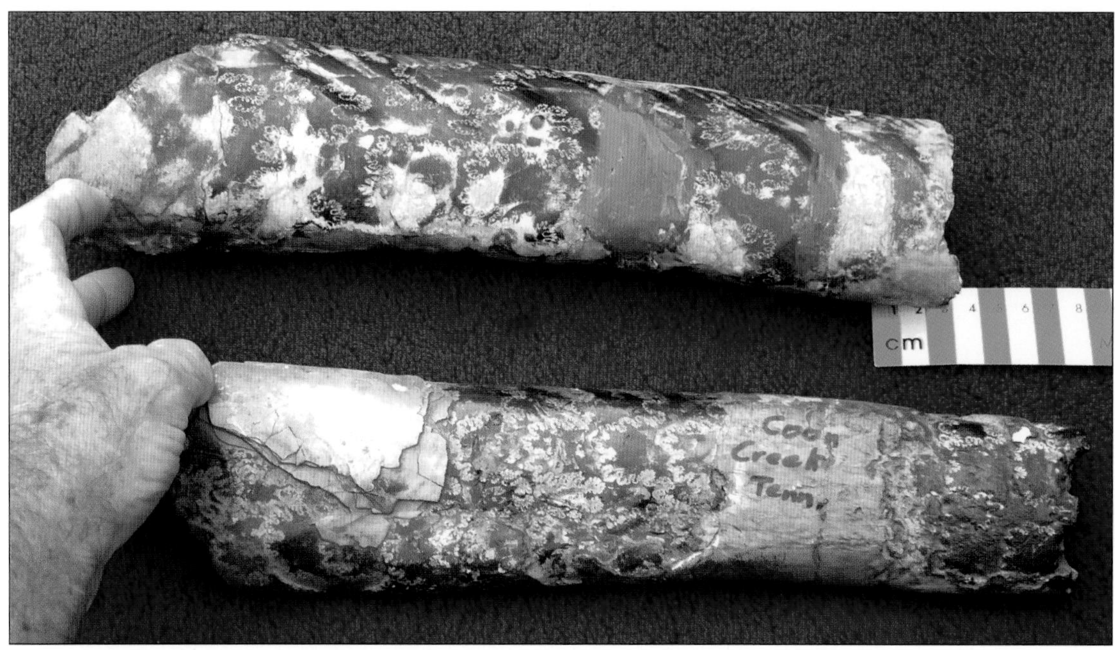

Figure 04-043. *Baculites grandis* Wade. A species of *Baculites* from late Cretaceous sediments of the Gulf Series. Coon Creek Formation, Ripley Group, Coon Creek, Tennessee. (Value range D, single specimen).

Figure 04-044. *Baculites carinatus* Morton. One of the last of the ammonites, a species of *Baculites* showing pronounced nodes. Owl Creek Formation, Owl Creek, Mississippi.

Figure 04-045. *Baculites carinatus*. Small specimens of this last species of Baculites species, which lived just prior to the Mesozoic extinctions. These internal molds came from the Owl Creek Formation in Stoddard County, Missouri, where the Gulf of Mexico came within 100 miles of St. Louis, Missouri. (Value range G).

Figure 04-046. *Gastrochaema* sp. Small, interior molds or shells of this pelecypod can be difficult to distinguish from small specimens of Baculites. This is one of a number of aberrant pelecypods which go extinct at the K-T boundary. Owl Creek Formation, Ardeola, Missouri. (Value range F, group of specimens).

Figure 04-047. *Baculites* sp. This is the living chamber of a small specimen of *Baculites,* which has been filled and preserved with quartz. This fossil was found in Missouri River gravels in the St. Louis area, having been transported at least 400 miles by river as there are no late Cretaceous rocks closer than this upstream from St. Louis. (Unusual, value range F).

Figure 04-048. Alaskan ammonite group. This is a superb group of Late Cretaceous (Campanian and Maastrichtian) ammonites from Alaska. Large parts of Alaska's mountain ranges are composed of Cretaceous rocks, much of which is highly folded and contorted and some of deep-sea origin. Many of these ammonites came from deep-sea sediments where they occur somewhat sporadically, their collection requiring lengthy traverses over the rough terrain of the Alaskan bush. As might be expected, the Alaskan ammonite fauna is still being added to—a situation which has resulted in extensive splitting of both genera and species of these ammonites. Variations in ornamentation, shell width to height ratios, as well as other morphological variations are being used to establish a plethora of genera and species. **Top row**: *Menuites* sp., *Pachydiscus* sp., and *Diplomoceras* sp., a heteromorph. **Middle row**: *Neophylloceras* sp., *Gaudryceras* sp. and *Nostroceras* sp., a heteromorph. **Bottom row**: *Pseudophyllites* sp., *Eutrephoceras* sp. (Note that this is a nautaloid and **not** an ammonite) and *Patagiosites* sp. These specimens were collected and identified by Curvin Metzler, an Alaskan resident.

Figure 04-049. Another group of Alaskan ammonites, *Courtesy of Curvin Metzler*. **Top row**: *Anagaudryceras* sp., *Damesites* sp., and *Desmophyllites* sp. **Middle row**: *Phyllopachyceras* sp. and *Tetragonites* sp. **Bottom row**: *Baculites* sp., *Solenoceras* sp., and *Naefia* sp.

Belemnites

Belemnites represent an extinct cephalopod order related to the living squid. Their mineralized guards can locally be common fossils in the Upper Cretaceous. Belemnites, like the ammonites, went extinct at the end of the Cretaceous Period.

Figure 04-050. *Belemnitella americana*. A late Cretaceous belemnite from Atlantic coastal plain sediments of the East Coast. Navesink Formation, New Egypt, New Jersey. (Value range G).

Figure 04-051. *Belemnitella americana*. Another group of belemnites from late Cretaceous sediments of the East Coast of North America. Navesink Formation, Big Brook near New Egypt, New Jersey.

Figure 04-052. *Belemnitella mucvouata*. A phallic-like belemnite from Campanian age strata near Hanover, Germany. *Courtsey of Naturmuseum Augsburg, Germany*. (Value range F).

Figure 04-053. *Niobarateuthis* sp. A distinctive guard from a large squid-like cephalopod. Niobara Chalk, Trego County, Kansas. *Courtesy of Scott Garrett*. (Value range E).

Arthropods

Decapod crustaceans (crabs and lobsters) are more commonly found as fossils in Upper Cretaceous rocks than they are in earlier Mesozoic strata. They are desirable and sought after fossils.

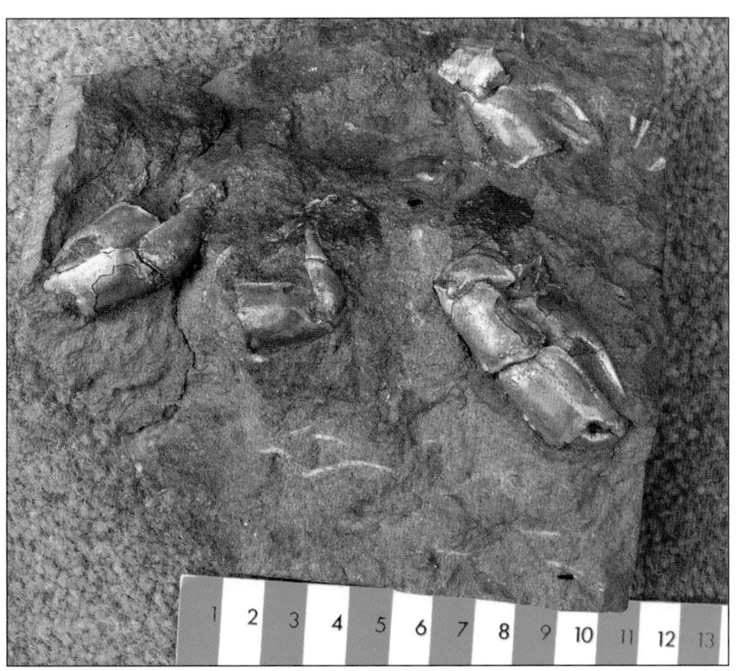

Figure 04-054. *Calanassa mortoni*. These ghost crabs are similar to small crabs of the genus *Calanassa* living today. They occur in groups like this in irregularly shaped concretions, which occur along the Ouachita River near Arkadelphia, Arkansas. (Value range D).

Figure 04-056. Burrow of a ghost crab, possibly made by *Calanassa mortoni*. Distinctive trace fossils like this are made by ghost crabs, animals which are still in existence today and which make similar burrows. Mt. Laurel Formation, Conn and Delaware Canal, Delaware. (Value Range G).

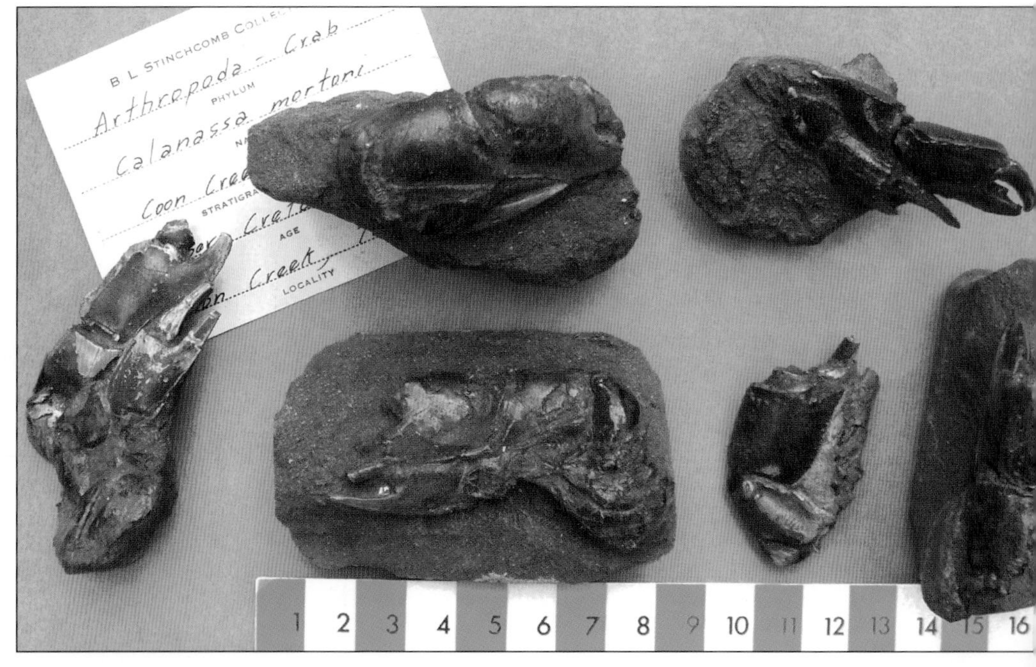

Figure 04-055. *Calanassa mortoni*. These are the same age and the same small crab as those in the previous photo (Figure 04-054). They are from the famous Coon Creek locality, southeast of Memphis, Tennessee, which is now a scientific preserve where the zone containing these crabs is now off limits to collecting.

Figure 04-057. *Dakoticancer overana* Rathbun. These crabs are from the latest Mesozoic, Owl Creek Formation, Owl Creek type locality near Ripley, Mississippi. (Value range F).

Figure 04-058. *Avitelmessus grapsoides* Rathbun. This crab is from the Coon Creek Formation, Union County, Mississippi. A number of very nice fossil crabs have come from various localities in Union County, Mississippi, which is south of Ripley, Mississippi, and the Owl Creek locality. (Value range C).

Figure 04-060. *Avitelmessus grapsoides*. Two specimens from the Coon Creek Formation of Union County, Mississippi, bottom left specimen from Coon creek, Tennessee.

Figure 04-059. *Avitelmessus grapsoides* Rathbun. This specimen is from the Coon Creek locality, Coon Creek, Tennessee. It is a life-like fossil that was found pretty well as it appears and required very little preparation. (Value range D).

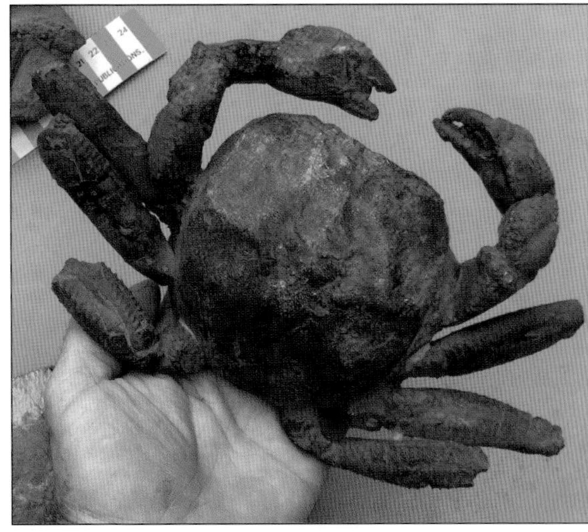

Figure 04-061. *Aveltimessus grapsoides*. A large, single crab from Union County, Mississippi. Large fossil crabs like this are found less commonly in Cretaceous rocks than they are in younger Cenozoic strata. (Value range B).

Vertebrates: Sharks

Shark spines and teeth become locally common fossils in rocks of the Upper Cretaceous. Shark teeth can be especially abundant as a shark can generate thousands of teeth over its life span.

Figure 04-062. *Hapolaria* sp. Lobster. These come from limestone concretions, which occur in the Bearpaw shale of north central Montana. Lobsters are arthropods but fossils of them generally are less common than are those of crabs. (Value range E).

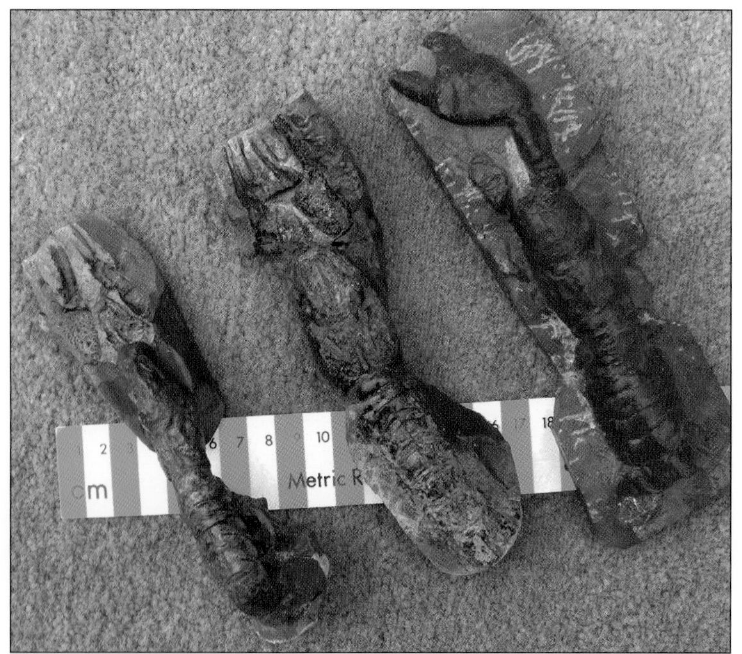

Figure 04-063. *Hapolaria* sp. Lobsters. Bearpaw shale, northern Montana.

Figure 04-064. Sharks' teeth. Eagle Ford Formation. A large concentration of these teeth was found in the Dallas, Texas, area in excavations for a shopping center. Sharks' teeth can be very common fossils, particularly after the Jurassic Period as a single shark could generate thousands of teeth, which they continuously shed during the course of its lifetime.

Figure 04-065. Sharks' teeth, mostly *Odontaspis* sp. The teeth of sharks become common fossils in Cretaceous and younger strata – but they are much rarer in earlier rocks. This is noticeable and puzzling since sharks go all the way back to the Devonian Period. Paleozoic sharks' teeth, in contrast to younger occurrences, are relatively uncommon fossils. Eagle Ford Formation, Greyson Co., Texas.

Figure 04-066. Sharks' teeth. Eagle Ford Formation. Another large group of sharks' teeth from Upper Cretaceous of Texas. SAFE (Save America's Fossils for Everyone) states, "Vertebrate fossils, being rare, should have legal strictures preventing their unauthorized collection." Fossil sharks' teeth, as well as some fossil fish, contrary of SAFE's statement, from the Cretaceous onward, can be some of the most abundant fossils, sometimes being more common than invertebrates such as snails and clams. These specimens came from an excavation in the Dallas-Fort Worth, Texas, area. (Value range for a group of twenty specimens, G).

Figure 04-067. Sharks' teeth can be locally abundant in Upper Cretaceous rocks deposited in the North American "Mediterranean" but are not as abundant in the sediments of the high plains, as they are in rocks of the Gulf Coastal plain where whole layers can be composed of them. Fossil shark teeth, which occur in the high plains, are the same as those in the Gulf sediments as sharks could travel through these different seaways, losing many teeth as they went. Carlyle Formation, central South Dakota.

Figure 04-068. These shark teeth come from phosphate rock which crops-out in the southwestern portion of Morocco. Specimens come from phosphate mines, which excavate into Cretaceous as well as overlying Cenozoic strata. A large number of these relatively large teeth, as well as vast numbers of normal sized ones, have come onto the fossil market during the past few years. (Value range G, single tooth).

Figure 04-069. The fossil sharks' teeth of Morocco represent various genera but are primarily of the genera *Lamna* and *Odontaspis.* They occur in large quantities in Moroccan as well as in other age phosphate rock deposits and have been widely distributed. (Value range G, group of specimens).

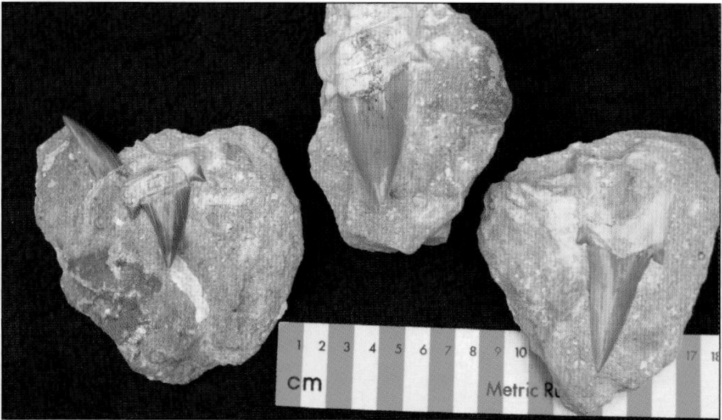

Figure 04-070. *Lamna* sp. A group of relatively large shark teeth from Moroccan phosphate deposits with phosphate rock matrix. Usually fossils in matrix like those shown here are more desirable than when the fossil is completely removed from the enclosing matrix. Oued zem, Khouribga, Morocco, phosphate mines, between Casablanca and Marrakech. (Value range F).

Figure 04-071. Shark coprolites. These are fossil excreta, derived from large sharks. Coprolites are primarily composed of calcium phosphate. Such phosphate material can contribute to the phosphate rock with which these coprolites are associated. Kem Kem Formation, Oued zem, Khouribga, Morocco. (Value range F, single specimen)

Figure 04-072. *Squatina* sp. Shark dorsal spines. These come from marine Cretaceous strata of Libya and were brought by locals to Moroccan fossil dealers. Such spines were located at the top (dorsal) part of the shark. Similar dorsal spines are found on the dorsal part of Paleozoic shark-like fishes (bradyodonts). (Value range F, single specimen)

Figure 04-073. *Protospyrina* sp. This is the dorsal spine of a large shark from the Smoky Hill member of the Niobara Chalk, Smoky Hill region of western Kansas. (Value range D).

Figure 04-074. The shark spine in Figure 04-073 was still in place in the Niobara Chalk when this picture was taken. The Niobara chalk was deposited during the late Cretaceous in a seaway (North American Mediterranean), which extended from Texas northward to the Arctic Ocean. Trego County, Kansas.

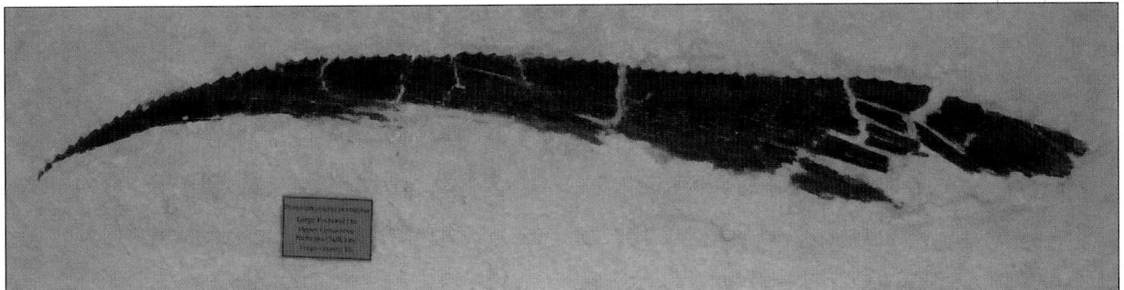

Figure 04-075. *Protospyrina* sp. A large specimen of this distinctive shark spine from the Smoky Hill member of the Niobara Formation, Trego County, Kansas. Large sharks that bore these spines may have preyed upon the predaceous fish found in the Niobara Chalk. *Courtesy of Scott Garrett*. (Value range D).

Figure 04-076. Outcrop of Niobara Chalk. Chalk is the namesake sedimentary rock of the Cretaceous Period and is named after the Latin word for chalk Creta (L) = chalk. This outcrop in western Kansas is associated with breaks and ravines of the Smoky Hill River, a major tributary of the Kansas (Kaw) River, which drains into the Missouri River at Kansas City, Missouri.

Peculiar teeth of sawfish and rays are shown here; rays are relatives to sharks.

Figure 04-077. *Onchopristus numidus*. Sawfish teeth. Tegana Formation, Kem Kem, Morocco. (Value range F, single specimen).

Figure 04-078. *Ptychodus latissimus* Agassiz, giant ray tooth. This tooth from a large, extinct stingray came from chalk outcrops in England where rocks of the Cretaceous Period were first recognized in the early nineteenth century. Lower chalk, Cenomanian, Eastbourne, Sussex, England. (Value range E).

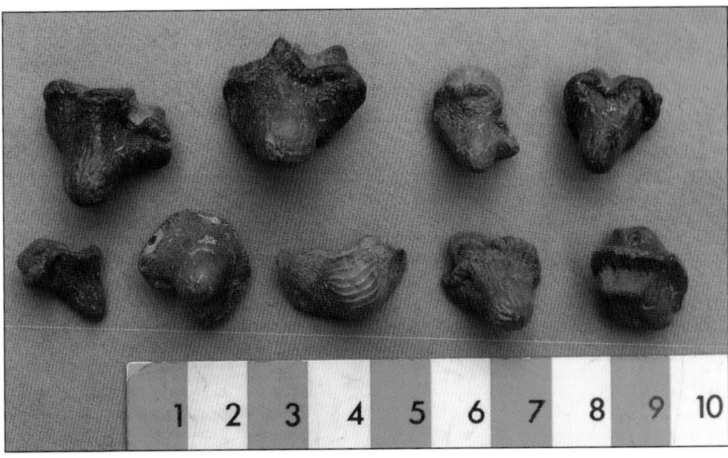

Figure 04-079. *Ptychodus whipplei*. Teeth of mollusk eating rays. Eagle Ford Formation (or Group), Dallas-Fort Worth area, Greyson Co., Texas. (Value range F for group)

Figure 04-080. *Ptychodus* sp. Greenhorn Formation, Butte Co., South Dakota. *Courtesy of John Stade*.

Figure 04-081. *Ptychodus* sp. Greenhorn Formation, Butte Co., South Dakota.

Bony Fish (Teleosts)

Bony fish became abundant in the Late Cretaceous. Some particularly large teleosts come from the Niobara Chalk of the North American high plains.

Figure 04-082. Fish (Sturgeon) in Niobara Chalk, Smoky Hill Member, Gove County, Kansas.

Figure 04-083. *Enchodus* sp. Fish jaw of a peculiar, Late Cretaceous fish found associated with chalk or chalky layers associated with shale beds. Niobara Chalk, Smoky Hill Member, Gove Co., Kansas. (Value range G).

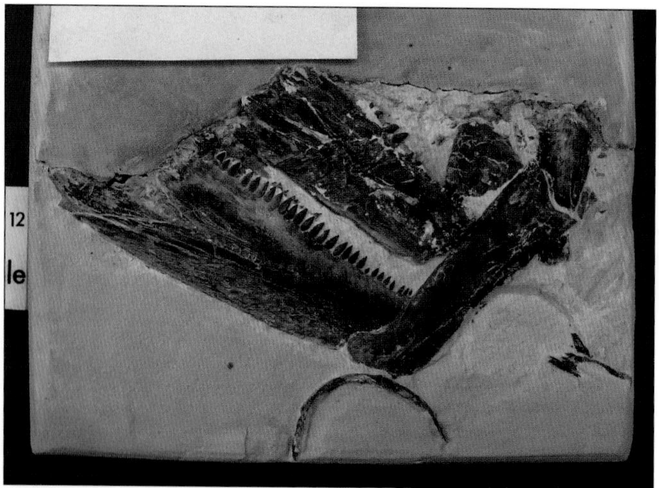

Figure 04-084. *Enchodus* sp. Jaw of a peculiar, predaceous fish. Niobara Chalk, Gove Co., Kansas. *Specimen courtesy of John Stade*. (Value range E).

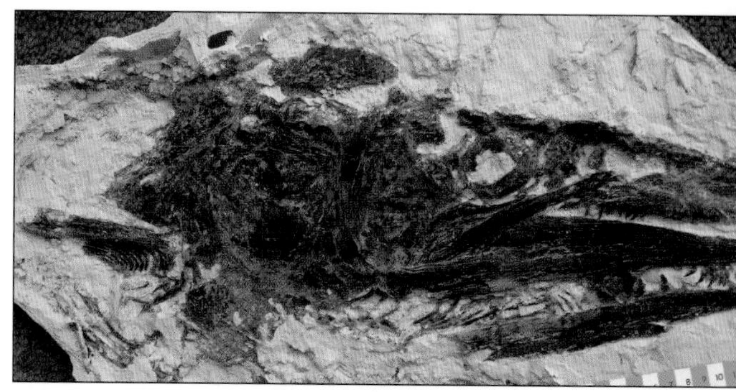

Figure 04-085. *Cimolichthus nepoelica*. A predaceous fish sometimes found as a fossilized victim of being eaten or bitten by a larger fish. Smoky Hill Member, Niobara Chalk, Trego Co., Kansas. *Courtesy of Scott Garrett.* (Value Range E)

Figure 04-086. *Cimolichthys nepoelica*. A more complete specimen of the same fish as above. Smoky Hill Member of the Niobara Chalk, Trego Co., Kansas.

Figure 04-087. A mounted specimen of *Xiphactinus (Portheus)*, pieces of which were gathered from chalk outcrops exposed in the grading for a highway in western Kansas. The rear portion of the fish is missing and a tail section of a smaller specimen found in the same area has been substituted resulting in this "head-heavy" fish. Niobara Chalk, Gove County, Kansas. (Value range C).

Figure 04-088. *Xiphactinus audax*. A superbly prepared skull of this large predatory fish from the Niobara Chalk of western Kansas. Specimen collected and prepared by Scott Garrett.

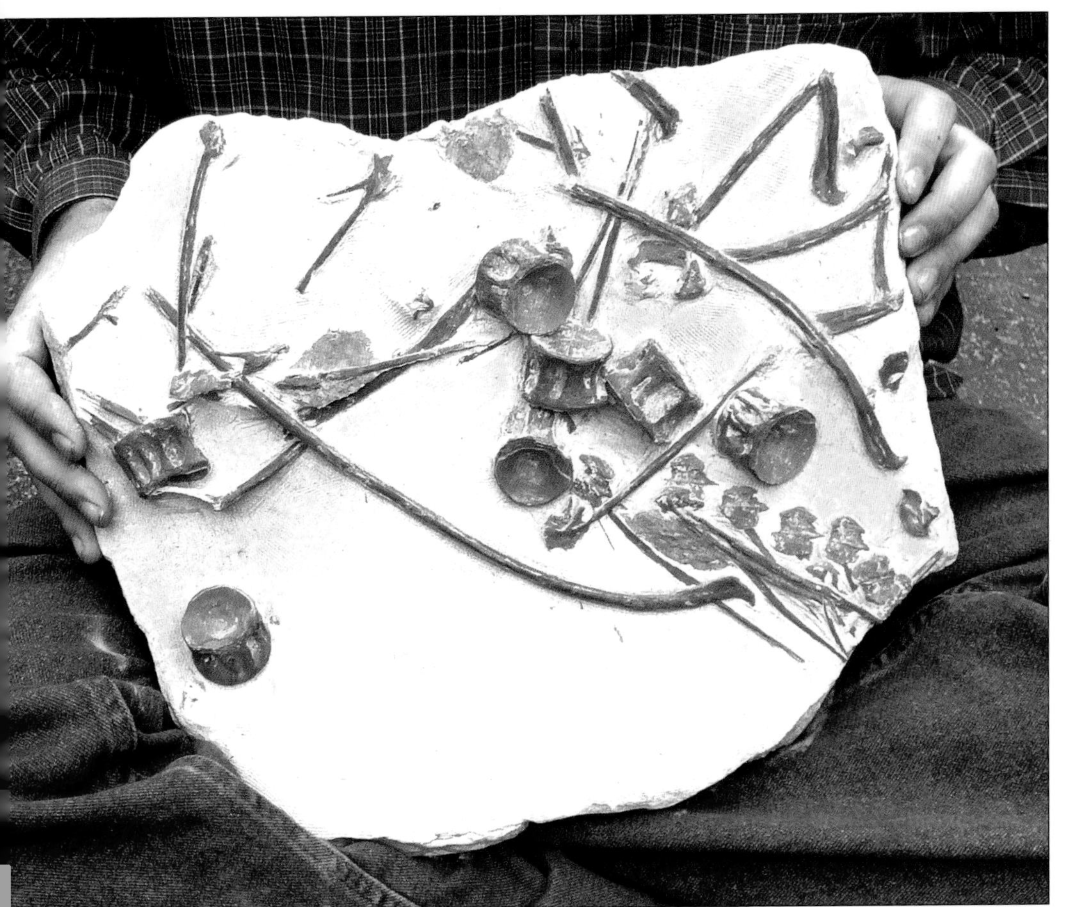

Figure 04-089. Slab of Niobara Chalk with a group of *Xiphactinus* (*Portheus*) vertebrae. *Xiphactinus* is a large predaceous relative to the modern tarpon. (Value range C).

Figure 04-090. *Xiphactinus audax*. One of the largest specimens ever found of this predaceous fish. Smoky Hill Member, Niobara Chalk, Trego Co., Kansas. *Courtesy of Scott Garrett.* (Value range A).

Figure 04-091. *Xiphactinus* (*Portheus)* sp. Specimen in grey chalk. Niobara Formation, Niobara River, South Dakota.

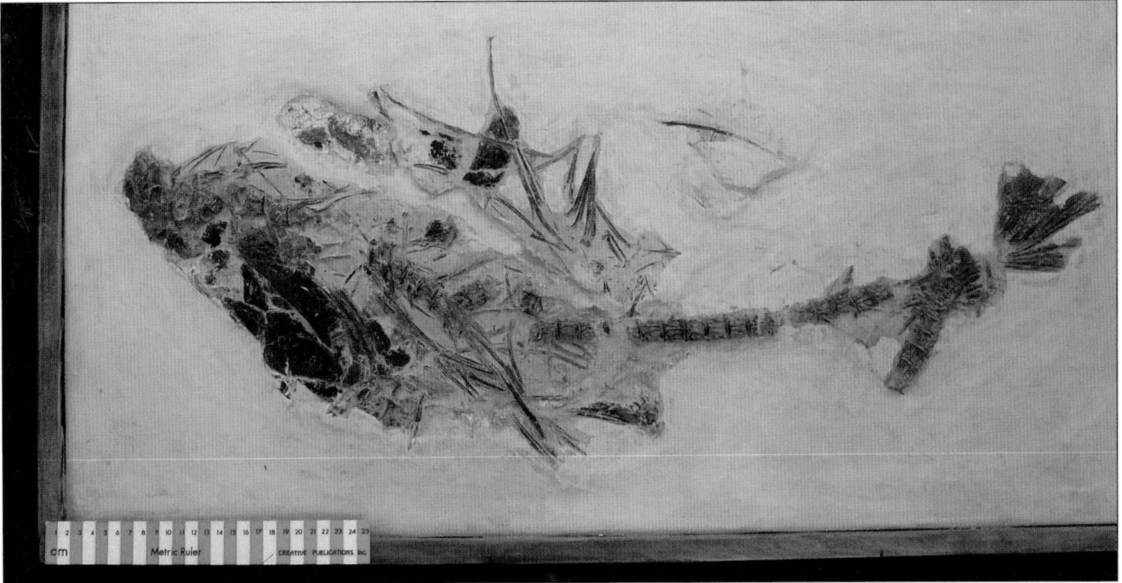

Figure 04-092. *Ichthydichtes* sp. Partial specimen of this medium sized fish in chalk. Niobara Chalk, Gove Co., Kansas.

Figure 04-093. Tail of a large specimen of *Ichthydichtes* sp. Niobara Chalk, Gove Co., Kansas.

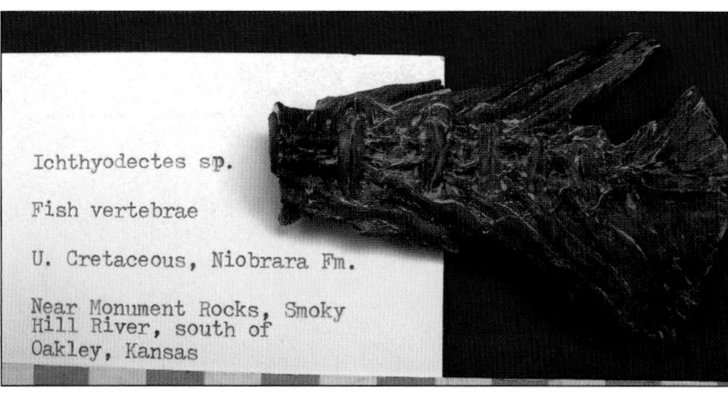

Figure 04-094. *Ichthydichtes* sp. Niobara Chalk.

Figure 04-095. Fin of *Ichthydichtes* sp. Gove Co., Kansas.

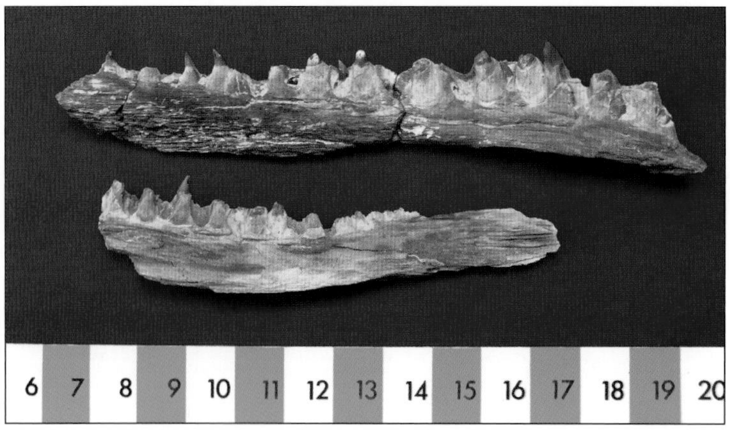

Figure 04-096. *Pachyrhizodus caninus*. Niobara Chalk, Gove Co., Kansas.

Crocodiles

The crocodiles were dominant reptiles of the Mesozoic and represent one of the ruling reptiles that escaped extinction at the end of the Mesozoic Era.

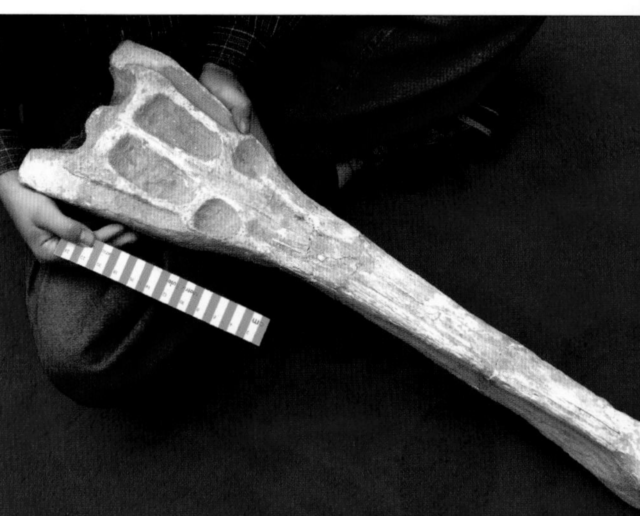

Figure 04-097. Crocodile skull, Moroccan phosphate deposits. Superb crocodile fossils are found throughout Moroccan phosphate deposits, which range in age from late Cretaceous to Eocene. Crocodiles survived the K/T extinction event and were (are) a highly successful reptile as they live and do fine today. Paleocene and Eocene crocodiles are very similar to this specimen, which could be younger than Cretaceous as the exact layers mined, and the age of the fossils salvaged from the various Moroccan phosphate layers are not well documented. The author was once told by a "scientific purist" that such undocumented fossils are utterly worthless without precise stratigraphic documentation. This seems to be a rather extreme position, which doesn't take into account the educational value of such fossils as well as their value and interest to collectors. Oued zem, Khouribga phosphate mines, between Casablanca and Marraketch, Morocco. (Value range C).

igure 04-098. Crocodillian jaw. Maastrichtian (?) phosphate leposits, western Morocco. Crocodiles are found throughout he Moroccan phosphate rock, which ranges from Late retaceous to Middle Eocene in age but most of the fossils ppear to be Cretaceous. (Value range C).

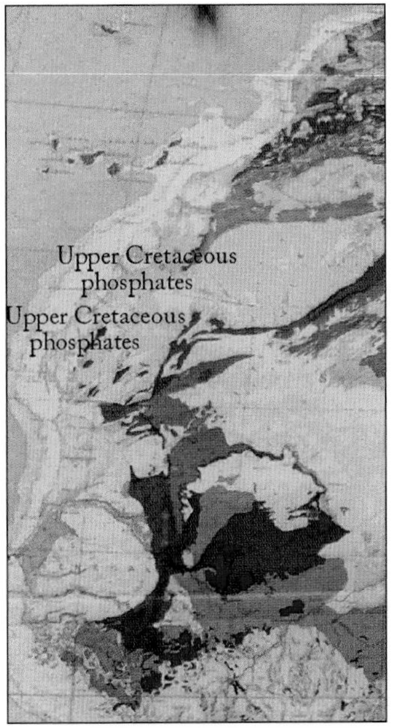

Figure 04-100. Part of the geologic map of Africa showing regions of phosphate rock occurrences in Morocco. Cretaceous and early Cenozoic, marine phosphate bearing rock occurs in the indicated coastal regions shown in light green and yellow east of the red areas in the Atlantic Ocean (Cenozoic igneous rock of the Canary Islands). The large green areas to the south are continental (freshwater) Cretaceous rocks, which yield dinosaur and crocodilian fossils including the teeth of *"Spinosaurus."*

igure 04-099. *"Spinosaurus"* sp. This is a group of distinctive eeth of the genus *Spinosaurus* sp. "Spinosaurus" teeth can ccur locally in abundance in Cretaceous sandstones of Aorocco, Mauritania, Algeria, and Libya. A large number of hese have come onto the fossil market through Moroccan ossil dealers and have been available during the past few ears at low prices. There is much debate over what type of animal bore these teeth. Some sources have **this type** of *Spinosaurus* tooth as coming from a mollusk eating rocodile; others consider these teeth as the teeth of a arnivorous dinosaur of which only one partial skeleton was nown as it wa destroyed during World War II. These teeth ome from fresh water deposits, which occur in badland reas on the edge of the Sahara Desert. (Value range F, single ooth).

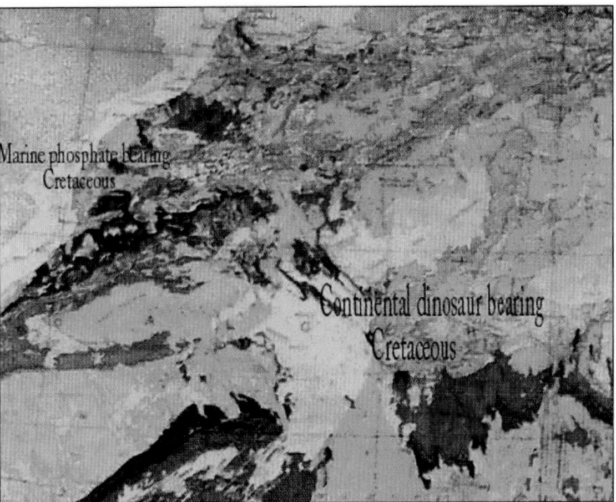

Figure 04-101. Another portion of the geologic map of Africa showing the phosphate bearing rock of southwest Morocco. The large outcrops (in dark green) of fresh water, continental sediments to the southeast are in Mauritania where dinosaur fossils including *Carachadontosaurus* teeth have come. This area is part of the Sahara Desert, where both fossils and meteorites are currently being collected by locals (nomads), which are sold or traded to Moroccan fossil dealers who then sell them at the large rock fairs such as those in Tucson, Arizona, and Munich, Germany.

Mosasaurs and Plesiosaurs

The mosasaur was one of the earliest ruling reptiles to be discovered—a complete skull and part of its body was found in a chalk quarry at Maastericht, Netherlands, in 1770. Mosasaurs were large marine lizards that apparently preyed upon the abundant ammonites of the time. Plesiosaurs also lived into the Late Cretaceous, although they were less widespread.

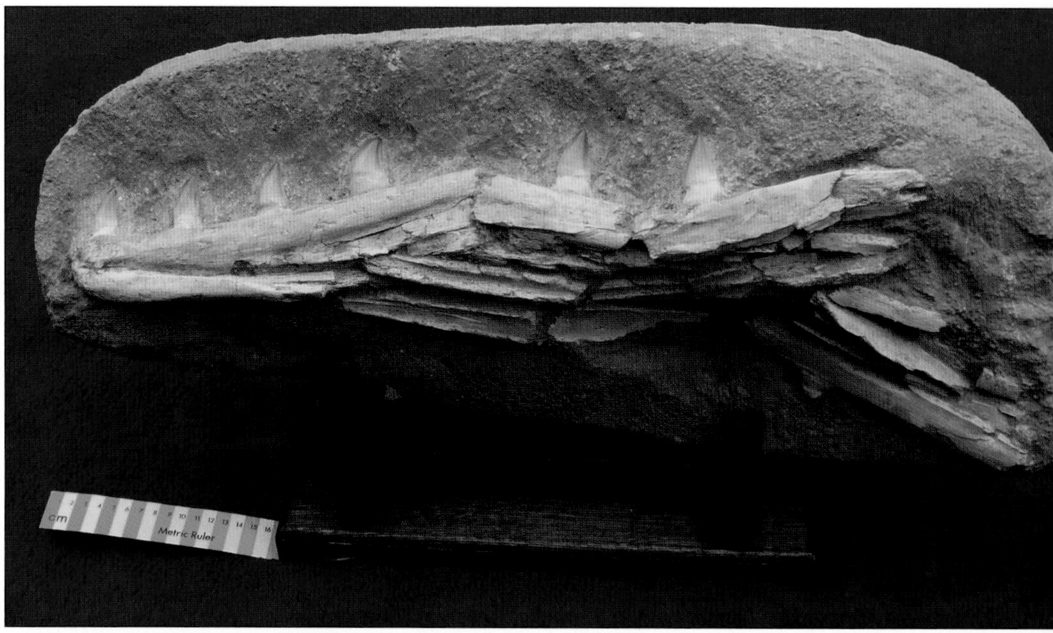

Figure 04-102. *"Mosasaurus"* sp. A mosasaur skull from Late Cretaceous (Maastrichtian) phosphate rock mined in southwestern Morocco. These phosphate beds range in age from Late Cretaceous through the Paleocene and Eocene with many of the sharks' teeth coming from Eocene beds. The Cretaceous phosphate beds also contain crocodiles as well as Mosasaurs. Crocodile and shark teeth from Moroccan phosphate rock, which appear on the fossil market, can range in age from Cretaceous through Eocene. The mosasaurs come from Cretaceous age strata, as mosasaurs were one of the fatalities of the terminal Mesozoic extinction, along with dinosaurs and other ruling reptiles. This is a superb specimen from Moroccan phosphate rock. It is somewhat similar in appearance and preservation (but smaller) to the original mosasaur collected from chalk beds near the banks of the river Meuse at Maastricht, Netherlands. Note the distance separating the teeth, a characteristic of all mosasaur jaws. Oued zem, Khouribga, phosphate mines between Casablanca and Marrakech, Morocco. (Value range B).

Figure 04-103. Close-up of the teeth of the mosasaur jaw shown in Figure 04-102. Note that mosasaur teeth are more highly pointed than are the teeth of crocodiles. Oued zem, Khouribga phosphate mines, Morocco.

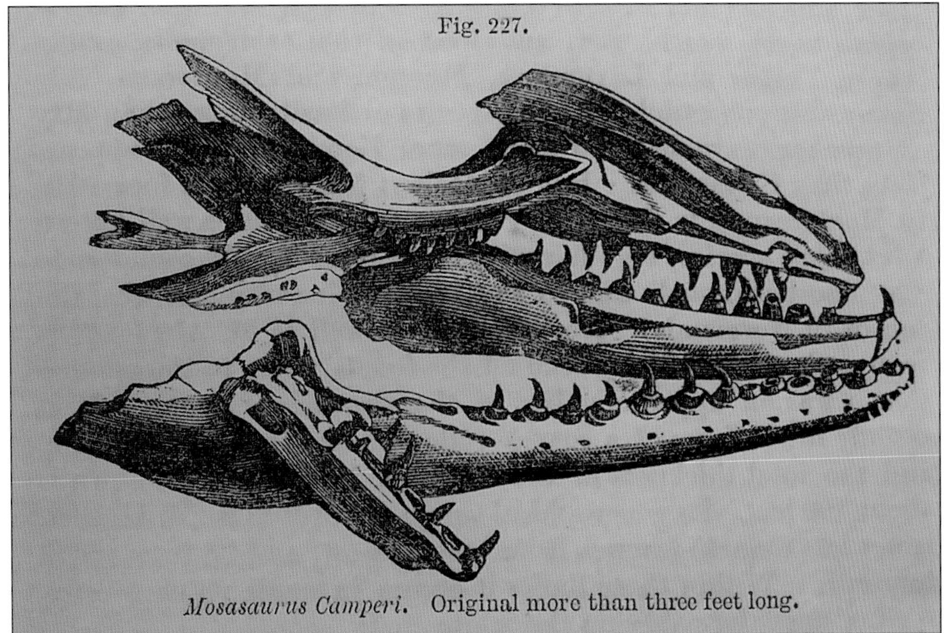

Figure 04-104. Illustration of the original type mosasaur from Charles Lyell's *Elements of Geology*. This skull was found at Maastricht, Holland, in 1770. The mosasaur was one of the first Mesozoic ruling reptiles to be discovered and recognized—ichthyosaurs, plesiosaurs, and dinosaurs came later in their discovery.

Figure 04-105. *Mosasaurs* sp. A mosasaur skull from the Niobara Chalk of western Kansas. *Courtesy of Dept. of Earth and Planetary Sciences, Washington University, St. Louis, Mo.* (Value range B).

Figure 04-106. Mosasaur teeth. Three examples of Mosasaur teeth from Moroccan phosphate deposits. Such teeth appeared on the fossil market at low prices and in abundance in 2004. Khouribga, Morocco. (Value range F, single tooth).

Figure 04-107. Single mosasaur tooth. Mosasaur teeth like this have appeared in quantity where they occur in phosphate rock. They come from Morocco. They also have appeared in quantity at the Tucson, Arizona, show during the past few years. (Value range F).

Figure 04-109. *Mosasaurus anceps*. A group of these robust mosasaur teeth in phosphate rock. Mosasaur remains, particularly teeth and jaw sections from phosphate rock of southwestern Morocco, have come onto the fossil market in quantity starting about 2002. Mosasaurs are a marine ruling reptile of the late Cretaceous but fossils are not always common. This material, from the phosphate mines of Morocco, represents a "bonanza" of mosasaur fossils. Such fossils come into the US through the Tucson show and represent an opportunity to get a specimen of this Late Mesozoic marine reptile at a very affordable price. Kem Kem Formation, Oued zem, Khouribga, Morocco. (Value range G, single specimen, very low price for such a nice fossil tooth).

Figure 04-108. Mosasaur teeth from Moroccan Cretaceous phosphate rock. The tooth in the upper left is the robust tooth of *Mosasaur anceps*; the others are the more slender teeth of *Platecarpus* sp. Oued zem, Khouribga, Morocco. (Value range F, single tooth).

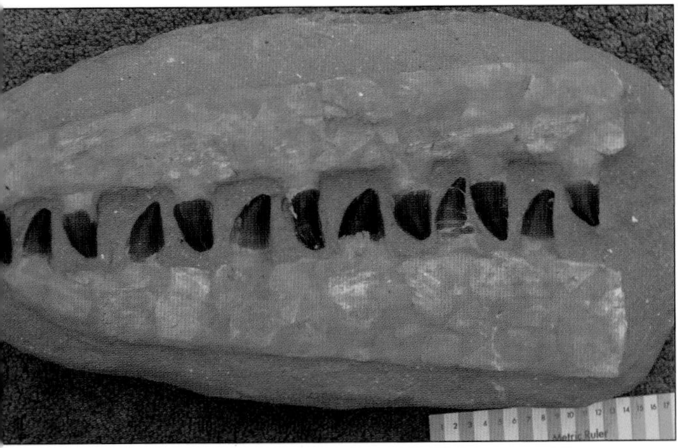

Figure 04-110. *"Mosasaurus."* A partially reconstructed jaw section of a **larger** mosasaur than that of above from southwestern Morocco. These jaw sections are **reconstructed** from mosasaur teeth and jaw fragments, which come from phosphate pits in southwestern Morocco. Mosasaurs, although one of the dominant marine vertebrates of the late Cretaceous, were predators and fossils of predatory animals are rarely abundant. In a way these reconstructed jaw sections represent paleontological "phony baloney," but they are made with real mosasaur teeth (usually) and they are cheap! In a more positive light, they represent an opportunity to acquire a spectacular Mesozoic fossil vertebrate at a low price, even though it's a somewhat inaccurate reconstruction. Kem Kem Formation, Oued zem, Khouribga, Morocco. (Value range E).

Figure 04-111. *Platecarpus phychodon*. Teeth from a smaller mosasaur than that shown in Figure 04-110. These teeth are generally offered as reconstructions with the teeth set in phosphate rock and a section of "jaw bone" added. Individual *Platecarpus* teeth generally fall out of the phosphate rock matrix and mounting them in this manner makes a more attractive specimen. Kem Kem Formation, Oued zem, Khouribga, Morocco. (Value range G).

Figure 04-112. *Platecarpus phychodon*. These teeth from a small mosasaur can be relatively abundant in the Cretaceous rock of southwestern Morocco. Locals collect the teeth from the mines and from piles of mined phosphate rock. The teeth are set into chunks of phosphate rock with mosasaur jaw fragments as can be seen below. The teeth to the right of the reconstructed jaw sections are those of Plesiosaurs, both come from phosphate rock of southwestern Morocco. These teeth occur in relative abundance and offer an opportunity for the collector to have a tooth of a Mesozoic ruling reptile. (Value range G, single specimen).

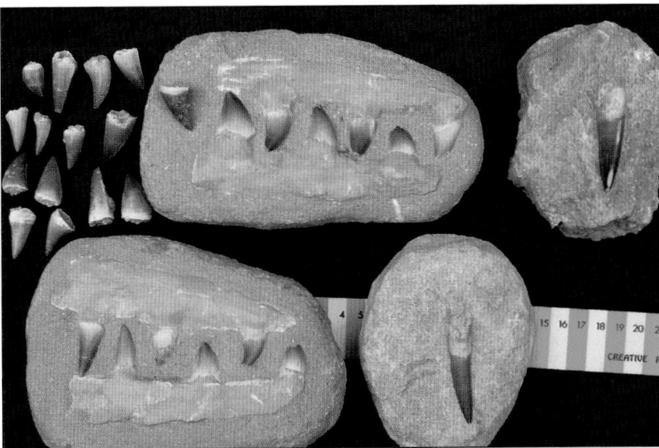

Figure 04-113. *Plesiosaurus mauretanicus*. Plesiosaur teeth, right. These slender teeth come from Late Cretaceous plesiosaurs. The jaw reconstructions are from mosasaurs. Plesiosaurs represent the other extinct marine reptile that was locally abundant in the late Cretaceous. Plesiosaurs however, are generally rarer than mosasaur remains and Moroccan phosphate-rock fossils offer an opportunity to own a specimen of what is otherwise a relatively rare fossil. Kem Kem Formation, Oued zem, Khouribga phosphate mines, southwestern Morocco. (Value range F).

Figure 04-114. *Plesiosaurus mauretanicus*. A group of Plesiosaur teeth in phosphate rock matrix. Kem Kem Formation, Oued zum, Khouribga phosphate mines. (Value range F, single tooth).

Figure 04-115. Another group of nice Moroccan Plesiosaur teeth.

Figure 04-116. *Plesiosaurus mauretanicus*. A reconstructed jaw section made up of plesiosaur teeth. Specimens similar to this have been distributed worldwide. They are reconstructed from teeth and jaw sections, which come from the phosphate mines of southwestern Morocco. Such reconstructed fossils are sneered at by some collectors, however they sell at a low price and do represent, if somewhat inaccurately, the jaw section of a Mesozoic reptile composed of real fossil teeth from a Mesozoic "ruling reptile." Kem Kem Formation, Oued zem, Khouribga, Morocco. (Value range G).

Figure 04-117. Specimen of the heteromorph ammonite *Baculites* sp. showing tooth impressions probably made by a mosasaur. Ammonites found in late Cretaceous rocks which have circular holes in them are believed to be the bite marks of mosasaurs. Mosasaurs appeared to have preyed upon ammonites with some regularity, as such "bite marks" are not rare. (Value range E).

Figure 04-118. A large specimen of the coiled ammonite *Placenticeras,* showing a series of holes believed to be bite marks from a mosasaur. Bearpaw Shale, Forsyth, Montana. (Value range E).

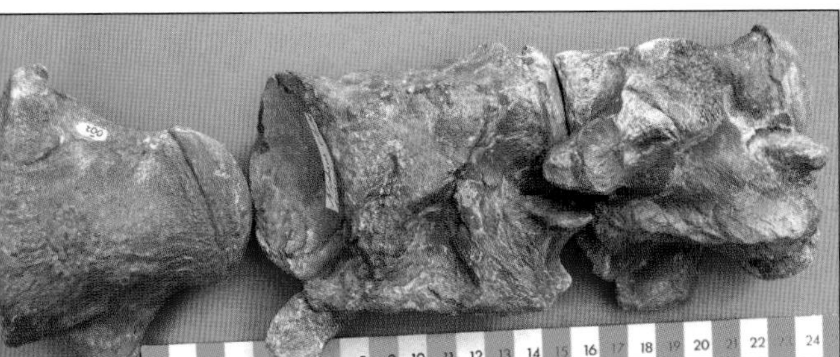

Figure 04-119. *Tylosaurus proriger* (Cope). Three vertebrae of a larger mosasaur, Niobara Chalk, Kansas. Individual vertebrae or groups of them can be found with some regularity in marine Cretaceous rocks deposited in the "North American Mediterranean" like the Niobara Chalk of western Kansas. (Value range F, for three).

Figure 04-120. Mosasaur vertebrae with a pronounced central process; such vertebrae were from the mid part of this large marine lizard. Bearpaw Shale, Kaycee, Wyoming. (Value range F).

Figure 04-121. *Clidastes* sp. Mosasaur vertebrae. Owl Creek Formation, Ardeola, Missouri. A scattering of mosasaur remains have been found in late Cretaceous rocks at the head of the Gulf Coast embayment in Missouri. These vertebrae are from the tail section of this large, marine lizard. (Value range F, rare occurrence).

Figure 04-122. *Clidastes* sp. Fragment of mosasaur jaw (South Dakota). The Pierre Shale, a thick shale sequence in South Dakota, Nebraska, and Wyoming, beside being the source of many fine ammonites, also yields mosasaur fossils. The relatively sharp teeth of this mosasaur jaw have been broken and eroded from the jaw section. Pierre Shale near Yankton, South Dakota.

Figure 04-123. *Tylosaurus* sp. A complete mosasaur from the Niobara Chalk of Kansas, Sternberg Museum, Hayes, Kansas.

Figure 04-125. Bronze model of a mosasaur from a set sold at the American Museum of Natural History; one of the usual offerings in "dinosaur model" sets. These bronze models have become collectible among "dinosaur model collectors" and now can be quite pricey. (Value range D).

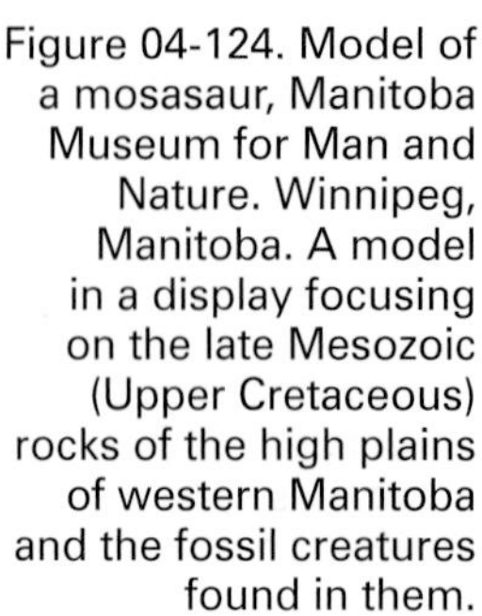

Figure 04-124. Model of a mosasaur, Manitoba Museum for Man and Nature. Winnipeg, Manitoba. A model in a display focusing on the late Mesozoic (Upper Cretaceous) rocks of the high plains of western Manitoba and the fossil creatures found in them.

Turtles

Turtles first appeared in the late Triassic. They can be locally common fossils in Upper Cretaceous strata of both marine and freshwater origin.

Bibliography

Larson, Neal, Steven D. Jorgensen, Robert A. Farrar and Peter L. Larson, 1997. *Ammonites and Other Cephalopods of the Pierre Seaway—Identification Guide*. Geoscience Press, Tucson, Arizona.

Stephenson, Lloyd William, 1955. "Owl Creek (Upper Cretaceous) fossils from Crowley's Ridge, southeastern Missouri." *U. S. Geological Survey Professional Paper 274-E*. US Government Printing Office, Washington D.C.

Figure 04-126. Sea turtle skull, Moroccan phosphate deposits. Upper Cretaceous (and early Cenozoic) phosphate rock is extensively mined in the southwestern portion of Morocco. Very nice vertebrate fossils from these phosphate mines have come onto the fossil market starting around 1997. Their availability from the extensive mining operations in the area located between Casablanca and Marrakech has been a win-win situation for all, individual and institutional collectors alike. There also is a benefit to the people of the region where the fossils occur, where their sale brings in economic resources. Some vertebrate paleontologists have criticized this arrangement, as seemingly they would rather see such specimens go into the rock crusher than fall into the hands of private collectors. Oued zem, Khouribga, Morocco phosphate mines. Presumably late Cretaceous, but possibly Paleocene or Eocene.

Figure 04-127. *Toxochelys* sp. The coracoid bone of a large marine turtle. These distinctively shaped bones are characteristic of turtles. Navarro Formation, Sulphur River, Texas.

Figure 04-128. *Adocus* sp. Fragments of relatively large fresh water turtles can be common fossils in rocks deposited in non-marine environments of the late Cretaceous. These are from the Hell Creek Formation of eastern Montana.

Chapter Five
Upper Cretaceous-III

Dinosaurs and Other Mesozoic "Ruling Reptiles"

Here they are, the "headliners" of the Cretaceous Period and the Mesozoic Era! However, this being a work focusing on fossils and fossil collecting, it should be pointed out that dinosaur fossils are probably one of the least practical fossils to collect. They can be large (and heavy) and usually don't appear very attractive as in some ways "one dinosaur bone resembles another." Also individual dinosaur bones can be like pieces of a puzzle which, when you have more pieces available, can be more easily and accurately put together. If there were any group of fossils best left up to the realm of museums and institutions, it would be the dinosaurs. Fossil dinosaur bones range from vertebrae to skulls. Recognizable bones are generally more desirable than bone fragments.

The king of Cretaceous tyrants, *T. rex* is probably the best known ... and loved(?) ... dinosaur. These carnosaur bones of *T. rex* came through a program (Dinotrek) with the St. Louis Science Center where a group of teachers and other interested persons search for and excavate dinosaur fossils from Federal land in Montana.

Figure 05-001. Dorsal vertebrae of *T. rex*.—Hell Creek Formation, Jordan, Montana. *Courtesy Carl Campbell, Dinotrek, and the St. Louis Science Center*

igure 05-002. Dorsal vertebrae of *T. rex*. Lance Formation, ance Creek, Wyoming. (Value range F).

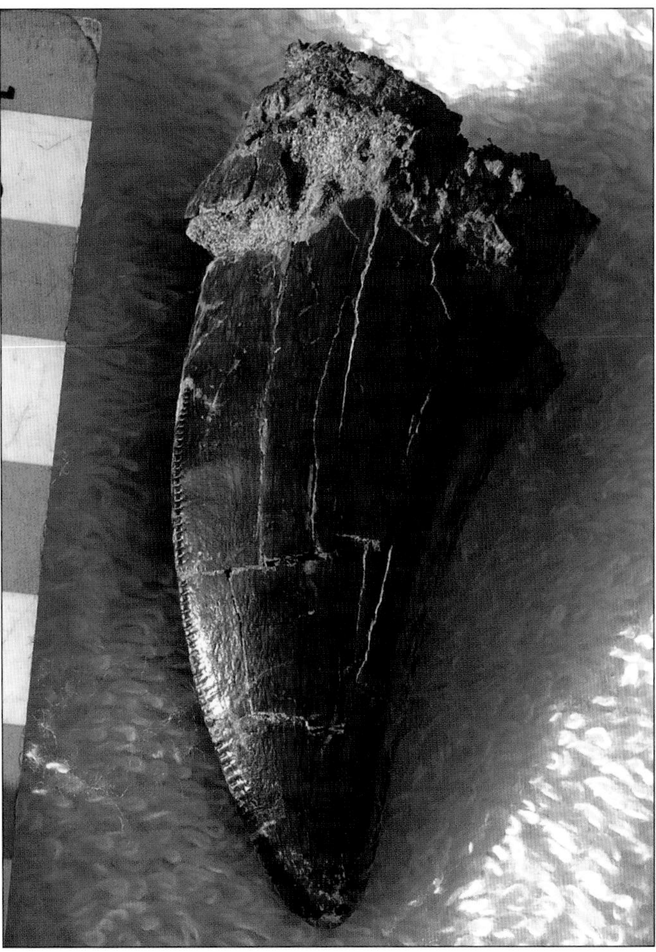

Figure 05-004. Tooth of *T rex*. Hell Creek Formation, Jordan, Montana.

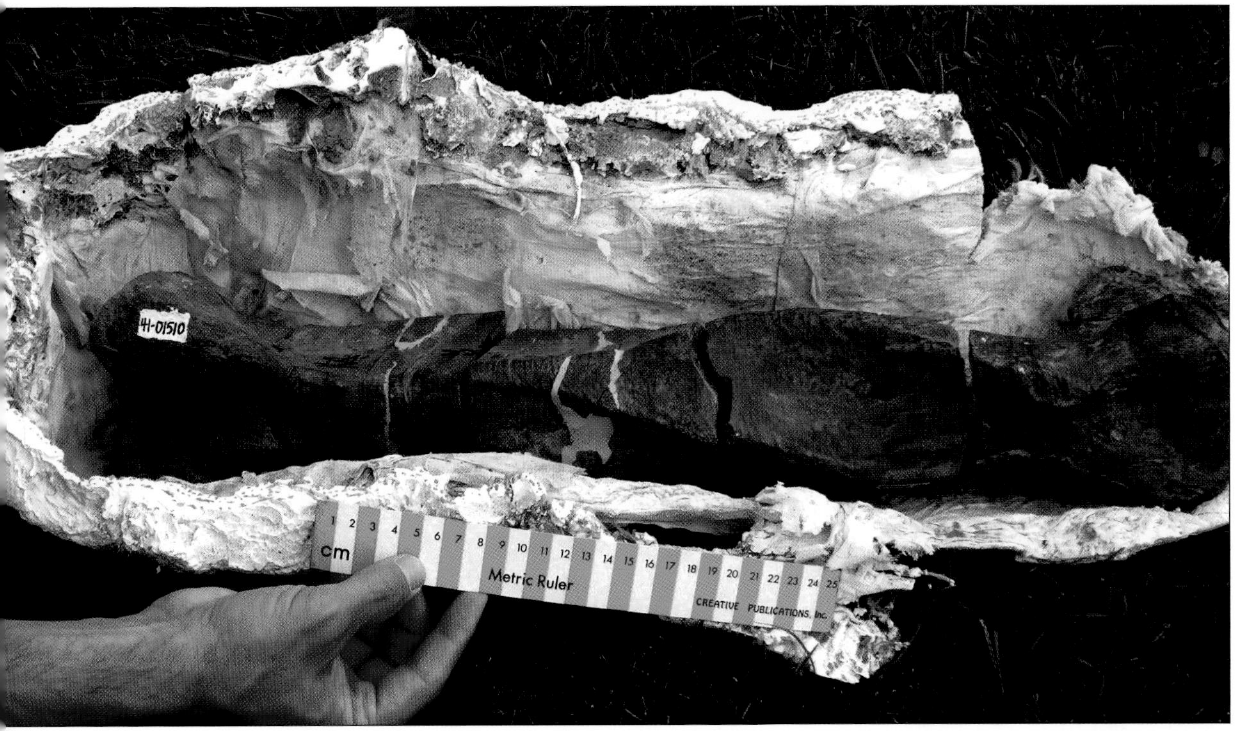

igure 05-003. Right metatarsal of *T. rex* (toe bone), Hell Creek Formation, Jordan, Montana.

These are the teeth of medium-sized carnosaurs from late Cretaceous rocks of North Africa. Extensive "badlands," similar to terrain yielding dinosaurs in western North America, occur in Morocco, Libya, Algeria, and other parts of North Africa. Carnosaur dinosaur fossils are relatively rare and these excellent teeth offer an opportunity to acquire some spectacular dinosaur teeth.

Figure 05-005. *Carachodontosaurus saharicus*. (teeth). These dinosaur teeth come from soft, Upper Cretaceous sandstones of southern Morocco and adjacent Algeria. These beds outcrop in buttes and badlands at the edge of the Sahara Desert and have recently (2007) produced new (to science) dinosaurs which have been featured in dinosaur-related cable television shows.

Figure 05-006. *Carachodontosaurus*. These three teeth once belonged to a carnivorous dinosaur (Carnosaur), similar to but smaller than *Tyrannosaurus rex* of dinosaur fame. Relatively large numbers of these teeth have come from arid Cretaceous outcrops (badlands) of Algeria and Mauritania where the teeth are collected by locals. Many vertebrate paleontologists bemoan such activity as associated with the teeth may be complete skulls or even complete dinosaur specimens, which would not be known of or collected by locals. Such indiscriminate collecting may remove "clues" to what may be in the ground for collection by vertebrate paleontologists and science. (Value range F, single tooth).

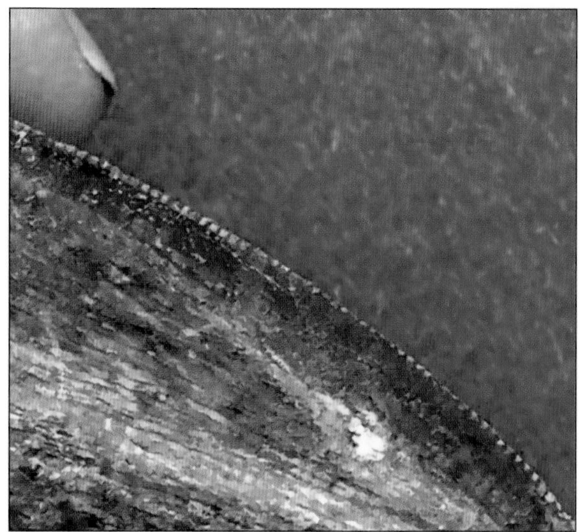

Figure 05-007. *Caracharodontosaurus saharicus*. Close-up of tooth showing serrations on the tooth edge. Such serrated dinosaur teeth (serrated like a steak knife) are characteristic of late Mesozoic carnosaur teeth and came onto the fossil market in some quantity between 2004 and 2007. Baharija beds, North Africa. (Value range F).

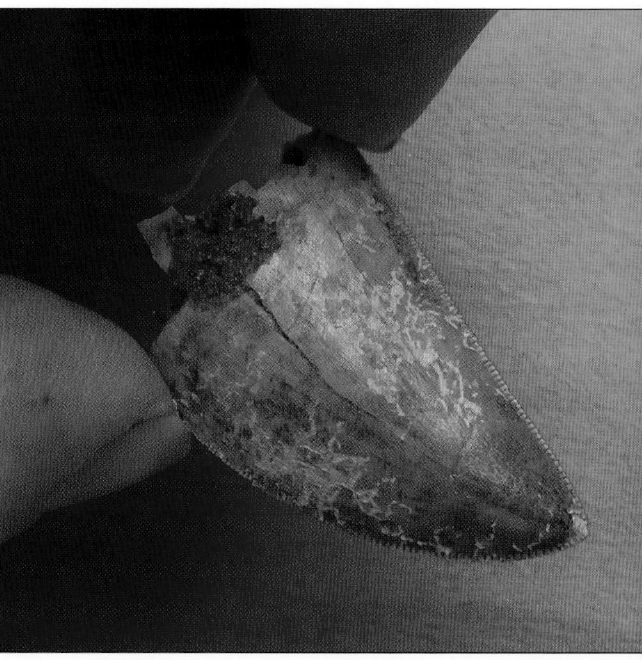

Figure 05-008. *Caracharodontosaurus* sp. tooth. Baharija beds, Albian stage, Kem-Kem Basin, K'Sar-es-Souk Province South of Taouz, Morocco.

Hadrosaur (duck-billed dinosaurs) were some of he most abundant late Cretaceous dinosaurs.

Figure 05-009. Hadrosaur tooth battery. The hadrosaurs, or duck billed dinosaurs, had a mouth full of flat teeth of a distinctive shape with which to engage in some serious grinding of gritty, woody vegetation, which included the fruit and seeds of early angiosperms. Lance Formation, Lance Creek, Wyoming. (Value range E).

igure 05-010. Portion of a hadrosaur jaw with tooth mpressions. Lance Formation, Lance Creek, Wyoming. Value range F).

Figure 05-011. Distal end (joint) of a hadrosaur femur. Upper most Cretaceous, west Texas. (Value Range F).

Figure 05-012. Hadrosaur (?) Femur lacking distal ends. Hell Creek Formation, Judith River, Montana.

Figure 05-014. Weathered skull of mineralized *Edmontosaurus* sp. Hell Creek Formation, Jordan, Montana. *Courtesy of Carl Campbell, Paleotrek, and the St. Louis Science Center*.

Figure 05-013. Hadrosaur vertebrae. Hadrosaurs (duck bills) were one of the most abundant dinosaurs of the late Mesozoic. As can be seen here, preservation of bones in non-marine, river deposits like the Lance and Hell Creek formations can have great fidelity. Note openings for blood vessels in this pathologic vertebrae. Lance Formation, Lance Creek, Wyoming. (Value range E).

Figure 05-015. Bottom view of *Edmontosaurus* skull shown ir Figure 05-014.

Besides hadrosaurs, remains of ceratopsian dinosaurs, particularly Triceratops, are one of the most commonly occurring late Cretaceous dinosaurs. Most of these came from the Hell Creek Formation of northern Montana and came through Paleotrek and the St. Louis Science Center.

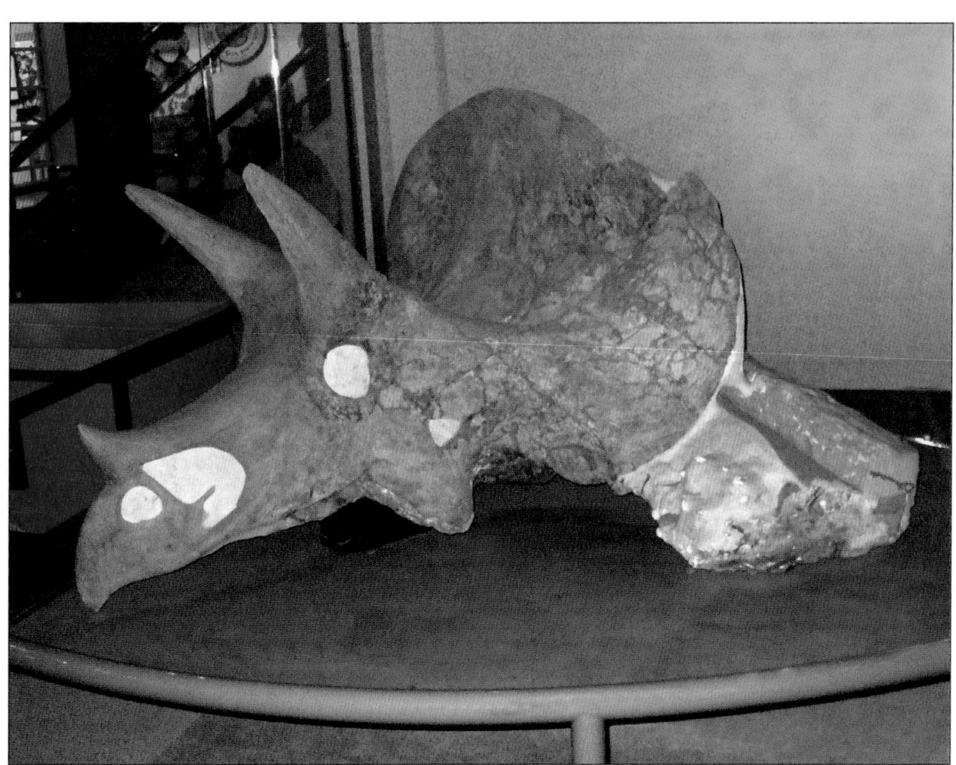

Figure 05-016. *Triceratops* sp. Skull of prepared specimen from the Lance Formation, Lance Creek, Wyoming. Specimen prepared by Guy Darrough and displayed at the St. Louis Science Center. (Value range A).

igure 05-017. Portions of frill or shield of *riceratops*, Lance Formation, Lance Creek, Vyoming. (Value range D).

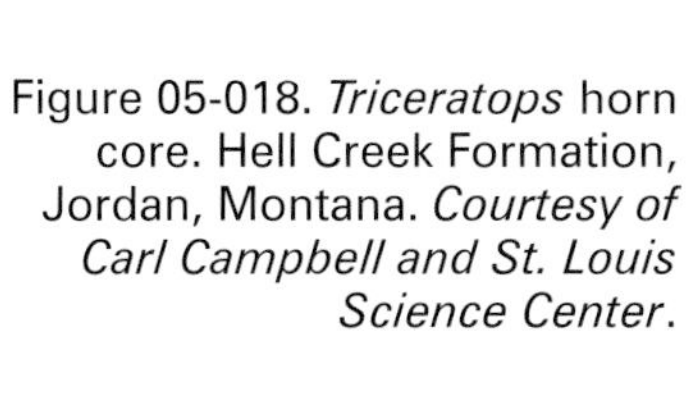

Figure 05-018. *Triceratops* horn core. Hell Creek Formation, Jordan, Montana. *Courtesy of Carl Campbell and St. Louis Science Center*.

Figure 05-019. *Triceratops* horn core (top) and occipital condryle. Hell Creek Formation, Jordan, Montana.

Figure 05-020. *Triceratops* horn core and partial frill (or shield) in outcrop. Hell Creek Formation, Jordan, Montana. *Courtesy of Carl Campbell, Dinotrek, and the St. Louis Science Center*.

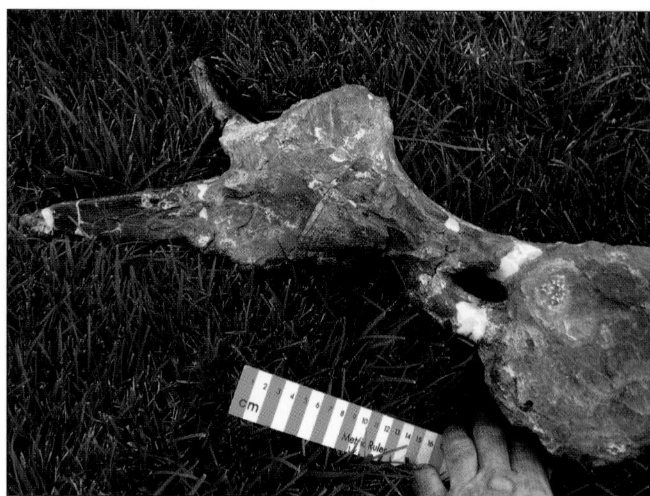

Figure 05-021. *Triceratops* dorsal vertebrae (with distal process). Hell Creek Formation, Jordon, Montana. *Courtesy of Carl Campbell and St. Louis Science Center*.

Figure 05-022. *Triceratops* dorsal rib. Hell Creek Formation, Jordan, Montana.

Figure 05-023. *Triceratops* jaw showing tooth battery. Hell Creek Formation, Jordan, Montana. *Courtesy of Carl Campbell and St. Louis Science Center*.

Figure 05-024. Same specimen as in Figure 05-023 showing outer side of jaw.

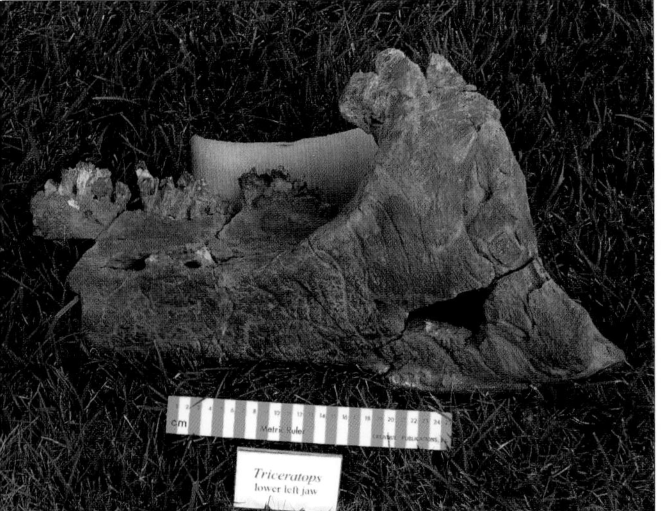

Figure 05-025. *Triceratops* (lower left jaw, somewhat weathered), Hell Creek Formation, Jordon, Montana.

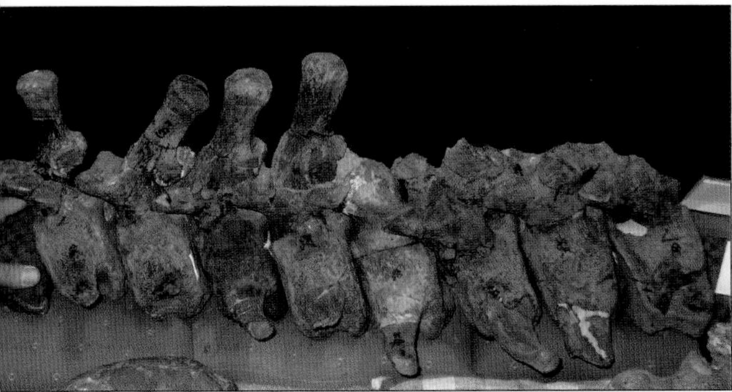

Figure 05-026. "String" of vertebrae from *Triceratops*. Hell Creek Formation, Jordan, Montana. *Courtesy of Carl Campbell and St. Louis Science Center*.

Figure 05-027. Single vertebrae of Triceratops from the Hell Creek Formation, Jordan, Montana.

Dinosaur Eggs

Dinosaur eggs have always been considered rare fossils. During the 1990s they appeared on the fossil market in quantity for the first time ever.

Figure 05-028. *Hypselosaurus priscum*. Dinosaur (?) eggs, France. These dinosaur (?) eggs come from red sandstone, which crops out in a grape vineyard in southern France. The rock in which they are preserved is identical to that which preserves most of the Chinese dinosaur eggs, that is fine, red sandstone. These French eggs have been questioned as to being true dinosaur eggs (*Science*, vol. 279, 1998). This uncertainty has arisen, as a consequence of large bones, believed to be from a large flightless bird, being found in the Langue dor region of France in the same geologic horizon as these eggs occur. These specimens came through Geological Enterprises, Ardmore, Oklahoma. Langue dor region, Aixen Province, southern France. (Value range D).

Figure 05-029. *Hypselosaurus priscum*. This is the egg shown at the left in the previous picture. Langue dor region, Aixen Province, southern France. (Value range D).

Figure 05-030. "*Oospecies*" (Therizinosaur egg). This is a group of the most frequently seen dinosaur eggs collected from Upper Cretaceous rocks of China. They are large and spectacular fossils on which some of the eggshell can still be present. One of the specimens shown here is **not** a dinosaur egg. Kaoguo Formation, Yisan, Huber Province, China. (Value range D, single specimen).

Figure 05-031. Therizinosaur egg. A specimen missing the eggshell. The shell is almost entirely missing from this specimen, its having adhered to the rock enclosing the egg when the egg was removed from the rock matrix. Such a specimen would be difficult for a novice to determine that it really was a fossil egg rather than being some sort of geologic structure like a concretion. Clues to its authenticity are small fragments of eggshell, which can be seen embedded in the red sandstone matrix, particularly at the edges of that part of the egg where the baby dinosaur apparently hatched. (Value range E).

Figure 05-032. "*Oospecies*." Therizinosaur egg. A specimen of a dinosaur egg from which the baby dinosaur presumably hatched. The top part of the egg is sandstone, which occupies that part of the egg whence hatched the baby dinosaur. (The egg was in the position shown when it was laid in the sands of a river delta). Other eggs from the same locality are complete, and are not missing the top portion of the egg. Such un-hatched eggs have shown, by the use of a CAT scan, the presence of small, faint bones of fossil dinosaur embryos. Kauguo Formation, Yisan, Hubei Province, China. (Value range D).

Figure 05-033. Therizinosaur egg. A typical complete egg. This is the most common occurrence of these Chinese dinosaur eggs. This is the bottom of the egg as the dinosaur mother laid it.

Figure 05-034. A group of "therizinosaur" eggs from China. Local farmers in China have found large concentrations of these eggs; they have been sold and distributed worldwide. Supposedly their export is now illegal, however numerous specimens entered the fossil market between 1987 and 2005 and at the time of this writing they frequently show up at rock and mineral shows as well as on the internet. Hubei Province, China. *Specimen courtesy of Stephen Riggs Jones*. (Value range D).

Figure 05-035. A fooler "dinosaur egg". This geologic object, known as lithophysae, occurs in volcanic ash beds and some of these objects, like that shown here, could easily be confused with one of the Chinese dinosaur eggs. Other geologic phenomena such as concretions and nodules also can be confused with and considered as "dinosaur eggs" by the novice. To evaluate whether a particular egg-like geologic structure really is a fossil egg (either dinosaur, pterodactyl, turtle or bird) requires specific information regarding its geologic occurrence as well as examination of the "egg" by a competent person. Most so-called fossil eggs **are not;** they are usually concretions or other such geologic phenomena.

Figure 05-036. Large dinosaur eggs. Some of the eggs from Hubei Province, China, such as these two large specimens have both the shape and size of a watermelon. *Courtesy of Bollinger County, Mo., Museum of Natural History and Guy Darrough*.

Figure 05-037. *Macroolithus yeotunensis*. Elongate dinosaur egg. These elongate dinosaur eggs came onto the fossil market in quantity in 1999. They are covered in an interesting article on dinosaur eggs in *National Geographic Magazine*, May 1996. (Value range B).

Figure 05-038. "Titanosaur" (sauropod) egg. An undetermined number of large dinosaur eggs from southern Argentina came onto the fossil market through the Tucson show in 2004. This is a crushed portion of one of these large eggs. These eggs are unusual in that they have often been filled or replaced with chalcedony, sometimes of an attractive translucent type, which resembles the whites of a hard-boiled egg. They are no longer available as the Argentine government has now banned all fossil exports. Rio Colorado Formation, Auca Mauevo, Patagonia, Argentina. (Value range F, single fragment).

Figure 05-039. *Titanosaur* sp. Dimpled fragments of a Titanosaur egg, an egg which is believed to have been laid by a sauropod. (Value range E).

Figure 05-040. A group of portions of quartz-replaced titanosaur eggs from Patagonia, southern Argentina.

Figure 05-041. *Titanosaurus* sp. (partial egg). A portion of a quartz replaced Titanosaur egg—the egg of a presumed sauropod. The outer portion of the egg has been replaced with chalcedony (grey), the egg interior has been filled in with crystalline quartz to form what is a (sort of) dinosaur-egg geode. Rio Colorado Formation, Auca Manevo, Patagonia, Argentina. (Value range F).

Figure 05-042. *Titanosaurus* sp. The outer surface of the egg fragment seen in the previous photo. A crenulated surface of the dinosaur eggshell (now replaced by chalcedony) can be seen. Rio Colorado Formation, Auca Manevo, Patagonia, Argentina.

Dinosaur Tracks and Trackways

As with earlier Mesozoic strata of the Triassic and Jurassic, dinosaur tracks and trackways offer a look at fossils made by living animals rather that dead bones, as is the case with bones and teeth.

Figure 05-043. Presumed hadrosaur trackway preserved as a natural cast on the sole of a large slab of sandstone. Frontier Sandstone, central Wyoming. (Value range E).

Figure 05-044. Tracks of small reptiles. These tracks are preserved on the surface of micaceous mudstone, which resembles the high-grade metamorphic rock known as mica schist. Small reptiles walked on a mud flat surface made up of small mica flakes, which came from an area of high-grade metamorphic rocks, probably the southern Appalachians. Ripley Formation, Ardeola, Missouri. (Value range F, single slab).

Figure 05-045. Trackway of a small animal, either a small dinosaur, bird or pterodactyl on a bedding surface made up of small mica flakes. Ripley Formation, Ardeola, Missouri (Value range F).

Non-dinosaur Reptiles

Non-dinosaur reptiles of the Cretaceous include turtles, snakes, pterosaurs, lizards, and crocodilians. Some of these reptiles, particularly turtles, can be common Cretaceous fossils, while others like snakes and pterosaurs are rare.

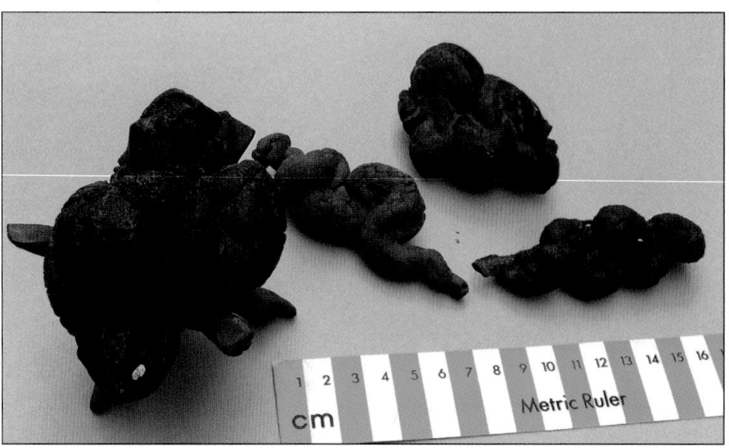

Figure 05-046. Coprolites! These mineralized coprolites are mentioned in various sources as being made by dinosaurs or associated with dinosaurs; however, they come from Oligocene age sediments of Oregon and are therefore considerably **younger** than dinosaurs. Dinosaur coprolites are not rare fossils, however they rarely look so "turd-like" as do these specimens. (Value range F, single specimen).

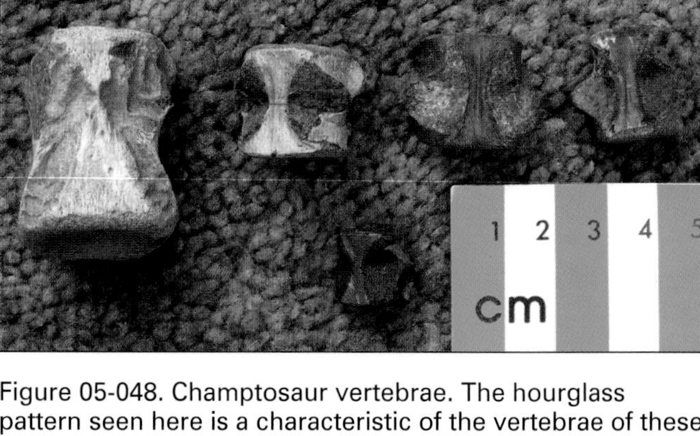

Figure 05-048. Champtosaur vertebrae. The hourglass pattern seen here is a characteristic of the vertebrae of these small, crocodile-like reptiles. Hell Creek Formation, Jordan, Montana.

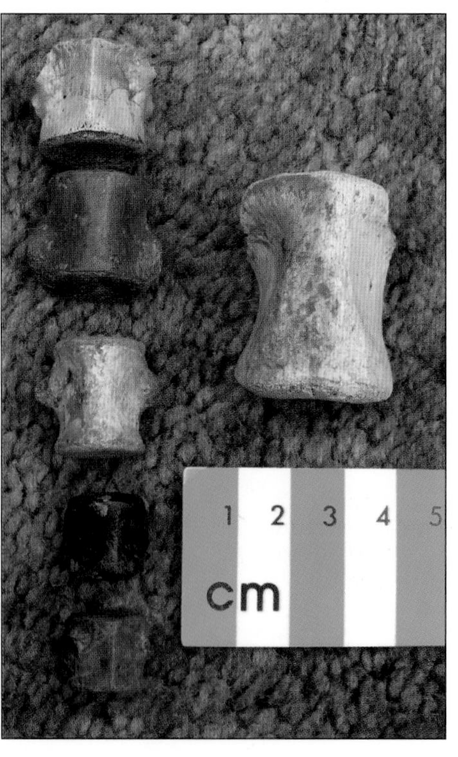

Figure 05-047. *Champtosaur* vertebrae. Champtosaurs were small reptiles that survived the Mesozoic extinction event (as did turtles, lizards, and snakes) but then went extinct during the Paleogene (early Cenozoic). Bones of these reptiles can be locally abundant in very late Cretaceous non-marine river deposits like the Lance and Hell Creek formations.

Figure 05-049. Champtosaur vertebra. A large vertebra of a champtosaur (bottom right) showing its characteristic hourglass pattern. Lance Formation, Lance Creek, Wyoming.

Pterosaurs

Pterosaurs were flying reptiles; they were **not** dinosaurs.

Figure 05-050. *Anhanquera* sp. Pterosaur tooth. Pterosaur fossils are rare as these flying reptiles lived only in specific environments and their bones were hollow and delicate and thus not readily preserved. Pterosaur bones can also be hard to recognize as such and complete, articulated pterosaurs are very rare fossils. This tooth, from a relatively large animal came from fresh water sediments of continental origin, which crop out in the Sahara Desert. It could be from Morocco as stated on the label but could also have come from similar beds in Mauritania or Algeria as both countries have locals who collect both fossils and meteorites, collectibles which they then sell to Moroccan fossil dealers. (Value range F).

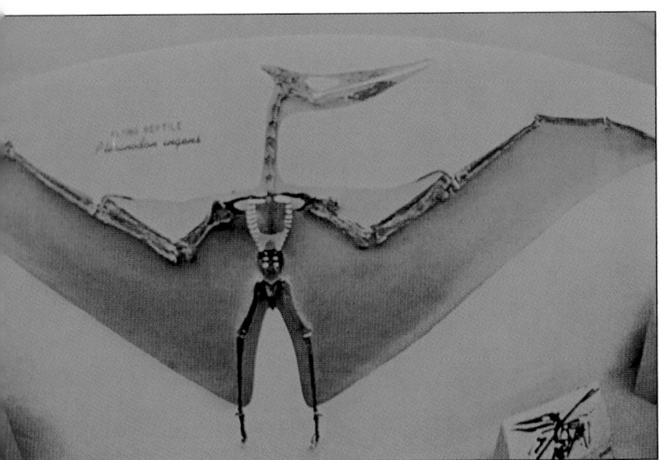

Figure 05-051. *Pterodon* sp. Hays, Kansas. This is a reconstruction of a large flying reptile exhibited in the Sternberg Museum of the University of Western Kansas, Hayes. The Sternberg's were a German family that homesteaded in western Kansas, in the mid-nineteenth century. A number of generations of Sternberg's collected, prepared, and sold vertebrate fossils they collected from Mesozoic rocks of the western states and territories. Large and superbly prepared fossils, collected by the Sternberg's, now grace many natural history museums of both North America and Europe. Pterosaurs were the largest of the flying reptiles. Isolated bones of a gigantic pterosaur have been found in the Rio Grande region of Texas, which was the size of a small airplane.

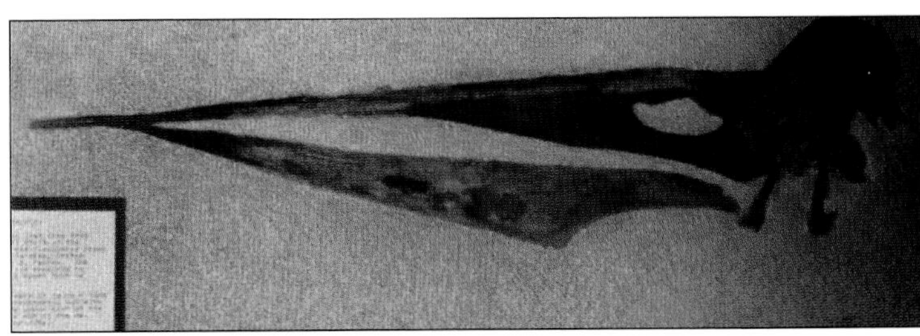

Figure 05-052. *Pterodon* sp. A skull of this flying reptile (pterosaur) from the Niobara Chalk of western Kansas. Specimen in the Sternberg Museum, Hayes, Kansas.

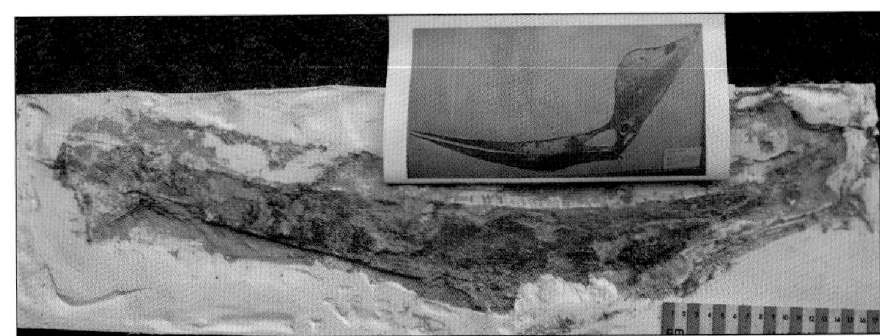

Figure 05-053. *Pterodon* cf. *P. sternbergi*. An unprepared and somewhat weathered upper part of a Pterodon skull. An image of a prepared skull of *P. sternbergi* is shown above the fossil. Smoky Hill Member, Niobara Chalk. *Courtesy of Scott Garrett*.

Figure 05-054. *Pterodon* sp. Fragments of a pterosaur from the Niobara Chalk. Individual pterosaur bones are usually hard to recognize and identify. They may go undetected by even experienced collectors. *Courtesy of Scott Garrett*. (Value range E).

Mammals

Mesozoic mammals are generally rare (often because of their small size). They are usually represented in the fossil record by their teeth. A Mesozoic mammal paleontologist is quoted as stating that, "Mesozoic mammal paleontology consists of one type of **tooth** evolving into another type over time."

Figure 05-057. Hadrosaur (model) lurking next to a rock and gift shop. Such advertising dinos were common local art in the western U.S. from the 1940s through the 1980s—southern Idaho.

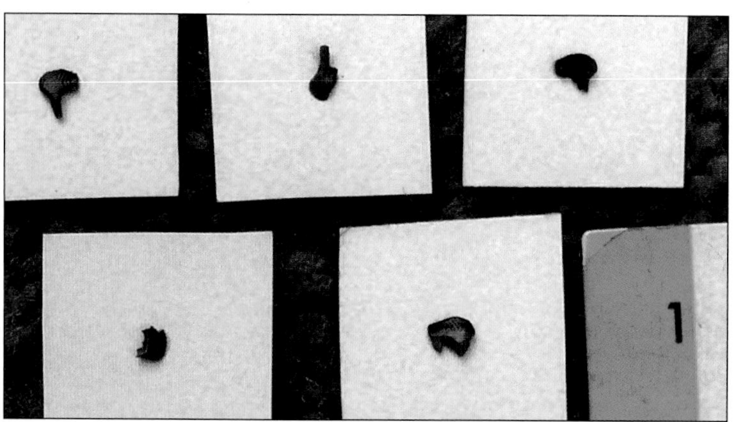

Figure 05-055. *Mosodea thompsoni*. Multituberculate mammal teeth. Mesozoic mammals were generally small and inconspicuous. These are the small teeth of small marsupials, which are found by washing large amounts of sediment from the proper geologic horizon. A concentrate of small rocks derived from the washing process is then picked under a microscope to actually find the small teeth. Hell Creek Formation, McHone County, Montana. (Value range G, single tooth).

Figure 05-058. "*Tyranosaurus rex*?" Another "folk art" dinosaur, this time a carnosaur waiting to eat some unsuspecting hadrosaur or tourist. Southern Idaho.

A Selection of Dinosaur Models

Kid's plastic dinosaurs are ***great***, but life-sized "folk art" dinos welcoming tourists are even ***greater***!

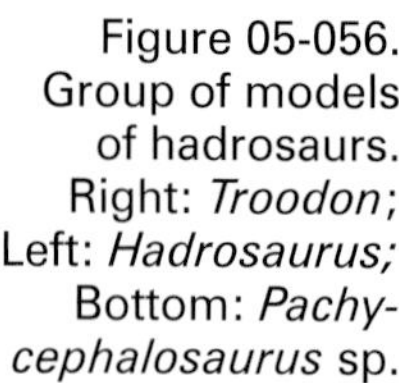

Figure 05-056. Group of models of hadrosaurs. Right: *Troodon*; Left: *Hadrosaurus;* Bottom: *Pachycephalosaurus* sp.

Figure 05-059. *Triceratops*. Oak Knoll Park. This fiberglass model at the former St. Louis Museum of Natural History met an unceremonious end when a tree fell on it during a storm where it was decapitated.

Figure 05-060. *Triceratops* sp. Plastic models of this late Cretaceous dinosaur which has been found in some abundance in Wyoming, Montana, South Dakota, and Alberta.

Figure 05-061. *Tyranosaurus rex*. A mix of cheap models of this favorite dinosaur. *T. rex* is found in continental (non-marine) sediments such as river deposits of Montana (Hell Creek Formation), Wyoming, and South Dakota (infamous Sue).

Upper Cretaceous Outcrops—Some with Dinosaur Fossils!

Figure 05-062. Mancos Shale outcrop (overlain by Mesa Verde Sandstone), Grand Junction, Colorado.

Bibliography

Ackerman, Jennifer, 1998. "Dinosaurs Take Wing." *National Geographic*, Vol. 194, No. 1.

Brochu, Christopher A., John Long, Colin McHenry John D. Scanlon, Paul Willis, 2000. *Dinosaurs* Fog City Press, San Francisco.

Currie, Phillip, 1996. "The Great Dinosaur Egg Hunt." *National Geographic*, Vol. 189, No. 9.

Gore, Rick, 1993. "Dinosaurs." *National Geographic* Vol. 183, No. 1.

Norell, Mark A., Eugene S. Gaffney and Lowell Dingus, 1995. *Discovering Dinosaurs in the American Museum of Natural History.* Alfred A. Knopf.

Ostrom, John H., 1978. "A New Look at Dinosaurs." *National Geographic*, Vol. 154, No. 2.

Rosenberg, Gard D. and Donald L. Wolberg, 1994 "Dino Fest." *Paleontological Society Special Publication* No. 7.

Weishampel, David B., Peter Dodson, Halszka Osmolsk, 1990. *The Dinosauria.* University of California Press. Berkley, Los Angeles, Oxford.

Figure 05-063. Mesa Verde Group Sandstone, I-70 western Colorado.

Figure 05-064. Niobara Chalk outcrop, monument rocks, western Kansas. Typical form of a Cretaceous chalk outcrop in an arid climate. Note the chalk pinnacle.

Figure 05-065. Illustration of a chalk pinnacle from the Cretaceous type locality along the English Channel. From Charles Lyell, *Elements of Geology*.

Figure 05-066. Pinnacle of Pierre shale along the Missouri River, central South Dakota. Where the little girl is standing are layers of volcanic ash (bentonite) derived from volcanic activity associated with the Laramide Orogeny; that period of mountain building which ended the Mesozoic Era and eventually formed the Rocky Mountains.

Figure 05-067. Outcrop of Pierre shale exposing vertebrae of a mosasaur. Central South Dakota.

Figure 05-068. Outcrop of Niobara Chalk overlain by Pierre shale. Missouri River (Lake Francois Case, South Dakota).

Figure 05-069. Marl exposed in a fresh road cut in southern Arkansas. Such marl can be full of fossil oysters such as *Ostrea* and *Exogyra,* but not at this locality.

Figure 05-070. Exposure of Upper Cretaceous limestone and marl (with fossil oysters) in an excavation at the east side of Tupelo Mississippi across from the boyhood home of pop music icon Elvis Presley. The site is now the location of a car dealership. Photo taken in 1960.

Figure 05-071. View of fossiliferous Cretaceous mudstone in southern Missouri (Crowley's Ridge). The white material at the top of the strata is bentonite, a type of volcanic ash. Late Cretaceous rocks worldwide often contain evidence of extensive volcanism, often from volcanic ash, which came from a considerable distance.

Figure 05-072. Close-up of the same outcrop as in Figure 05-071. The fossil is the high-spired gastropod *Turritella* sp.

Figure 05-073. Closer view of the Figure 05-072 image showing the internal mold of the gastropod *Turritella* in place.

Figure 05-074. Bedded, micaceous (mica-bearing) clay beds, which yield small vertebrate tracks. Crowley's Ridge, SE Missouri.

Figure 05-076. Severely folded and crumpled Upper Cretaceous strata of deep-sea origin. Little Tonzona River, central Alaska.

Figure 05-075. Folded and fractured Upper Cretaceous marine limestone of deep sea origin exposed along the Little Tonzona River north of the Alaskan Range on the upthrown side of the Denali Fault. These strata of deep-sea origin have been severely squeezed and crumpled. They contain few fossils and those that do occur are hard to spot.

Figure 05-077. Close-up of tight fold shown in Figure 05-076. The conspicuous layers are hard, iron-rich limestone beds.

Figure 05-078. Outcrop of Hell Creek Formation on BLM (Federal land) with excavation for dinosaur bones. *This and the following photos courtesy of Carl Campbell, Paleotrek, and the St. Louis Science Center.*

Figure 05-080. Dino bone pits on Paleotrek dig, Jordan, Montana.

Figure 05-079. Excavation pit in which hadrosaur bones were excavated. Hell Creek Formation, Jordan, Montana.

Figure 05-081. Excavating hadrosaur bones at Paleotrek dig. Jordan, Montana.

Figure 05-082. Same as Figure 05-081!

Figure 05-083. "Paleodog" in the shade of a Hell Creek Formation outcrop.

Figure 05-084. Hodoos and badlands carved from the Hell Creek and Fort Union Formations, Jordan, Montana.

Chapter Six

The Missouri Dinosaur Site

Scattered over the Ozarks of Missouri and Arkansas are localized concentrations of fossils, some of a geologic age alien to the region in which they are found. Such isolated occurrences of younger rocks are known as outliers and have fascinated many geologists, as they are a distinctive geologic feature characteristic of the Ozarks and the geology of southern Missouri.

Over the years, various geologists have documented a number of them, many of which are shown on the 1979 version of the geologic map of Missouri. One of the strangest of these isolated occurrences, one discovered and located in the southeastern Ozarks of Missouri in the early 1940s, yielded the bones of **dinosaurs**.

Figure 06-003. Hard rocks capping knobs, preserved in paleokarsts of Mississippian age just north of Rolla, Missouri, produced these fossils. These late Paleozoic fossils come from strata preserved in these ancient sinkholes. This "snail bearing" rock is considerably younger than most of the rock in the Rolla area, which belongs to the lower (or early) part of the Paleozoic Era.

Figure 06-001. An example of a small, localized occurrence of younger rock, this is a cross-section of an ancient, sediment filled sinkhole or paleokarst exposed in a road cut south of Jefferson City, Missouri. Such ancient, sediment filled sinkholes are a major part of Ozark geology and have been responsible for preserving sediments and sedimentary rocks of various ages which otherwise would have been eroded away long ago. Missouri's (only known) dinosaur site has been preserved in this way.

Figure 06-004. Isolated occurrences of rocks of Late Mesozoic (Cretaceous) age (green), Ordovican, and Silurian (pink) in a geologically complex area around Marble Hill, Missouri. The Missouri Dinosaur site (Chronister Site) is the green dot to the northwest (10:00 O'clock). Other Cretaceous outliers also occur in the area and some of these might also contain dinosaur remains. Such isolated occurrences of these younger rocks represent areas where ancient sinkholes (or grabens) preserved rocks with a greater thickness or hardness that otherwise would have been eroded away.

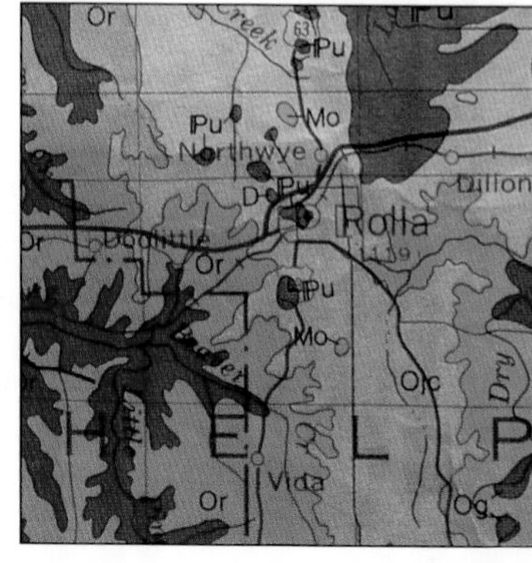

Figure 06-002. Part of the 1979 Geologic Map of Missouri showing isolated occurrences (outliers) of Devonian and Mississippian fossil bearing rocks around Rolla, Missouri. These isolated occurrences of younger rock strata, referred to as outliers, occur throughout much of the Ozark region of Missouri and Arkansas. They represent remnants of once more widespread rocks, which were deposited in ancient sinkholes (paleokarsts). Purple=Devonian, Blue=Mississippian, Grey=Pennsylvanian

Figure 06-005. Ozark Knob capped by brecciated (broken and re-cemented) chert, which is geologically younger than are the rocks at lower elevations surrounding the knob. This cap of hard rock served as a type of armor plate preventing rocks of the knob from being eroded away while the softer, surrounding rocks were worn down leaving this knob topped by its cap of younger, hard rock.

Figure 06-006. Hard, highly brecciated chert capping a knob (Nichols Knob) in Douglas County, Missouri. These brecciated (broken and re-cemented together) chert masses may have been produced during the Mesozoic Era from the impact of a fragmented asteroid. Rock flour, generated by the impact and composed mostly of quartz, cemented the chert fragments together to form a very hard rock which has defied weathering and erosion while the surrounding softer rocks were worn down. Such differential erosion left a cap of the hard-brecciated rock forming the top of the knob. Such remnants of younger rocks, often forming knobs like this, are a characteristic feature of Ozark geology.

History

Strata of Mesozoic age were unknown in Missouri prior to the late 1930s. In the mid-1930s, Willard Farrar and Lyle McManamy, working on a WPA financed program with the Missouri Geological Survey, geologically mapped Stoddard County in southeastern Missouri and discovered the presence of Cretaceous clays; this discovery was announced and reported in their 1937-Geology of Stoddard County. Interest in the geology of the southeastern part of Missouri continued with geologic investigations, which extended north of Stoddard County into the Ozark region of Bollinger County. Dan Steward, coming on with the Missouri Geological Survey in 1940, began the geologic mapping of an area in the vicinity of Marble Hill in the southeastern Ozarks. Geologic mapping of this area found a particularly puzzling or anomalous area of geology along Crooked Creek west of Marble Hill in 1941. In this area, Steward was shown a group of bones recovered from blue-clay, which was found when digging a cistern at the back of the house of Lula Chronister. Already aware of peculiar blue-grey clays in the banks of nearby Crooked Creek, Steward was open to the possibility that such clay might be Mesozoic (Cretaceous) in age since marine clays of that age had been found to the south in Stoddard County a few years earlier.

Taking some of the bones to Rolla, the home of the Missouri Geological Survey, "Chief Buehler," the state geologist at the time, reportedly barked out, "Why those are nothing but old cow bones." Convinced that the bones were definitely fossils and possibly even the bones of a dinosaur, Steward collaborated with Maurice Mehl of the University of Missouri (the only one at that time, the one in Columbia) to determine what he really had.

Figure 06-007. *Geology of Stoddard County*. Geologic reports on specific regions, like this *Geology of Stoddard County*, can be a source of information on the geology of a specific area, including local occurrences of fossils. In this work from 1937, the discovery of Mesozoic rocks in Missouri was announced. This discovery eventually led to the discovery of dinosaur bearing rocks further north in the Ozark area of southeastern Missouri. (Value range F for book).

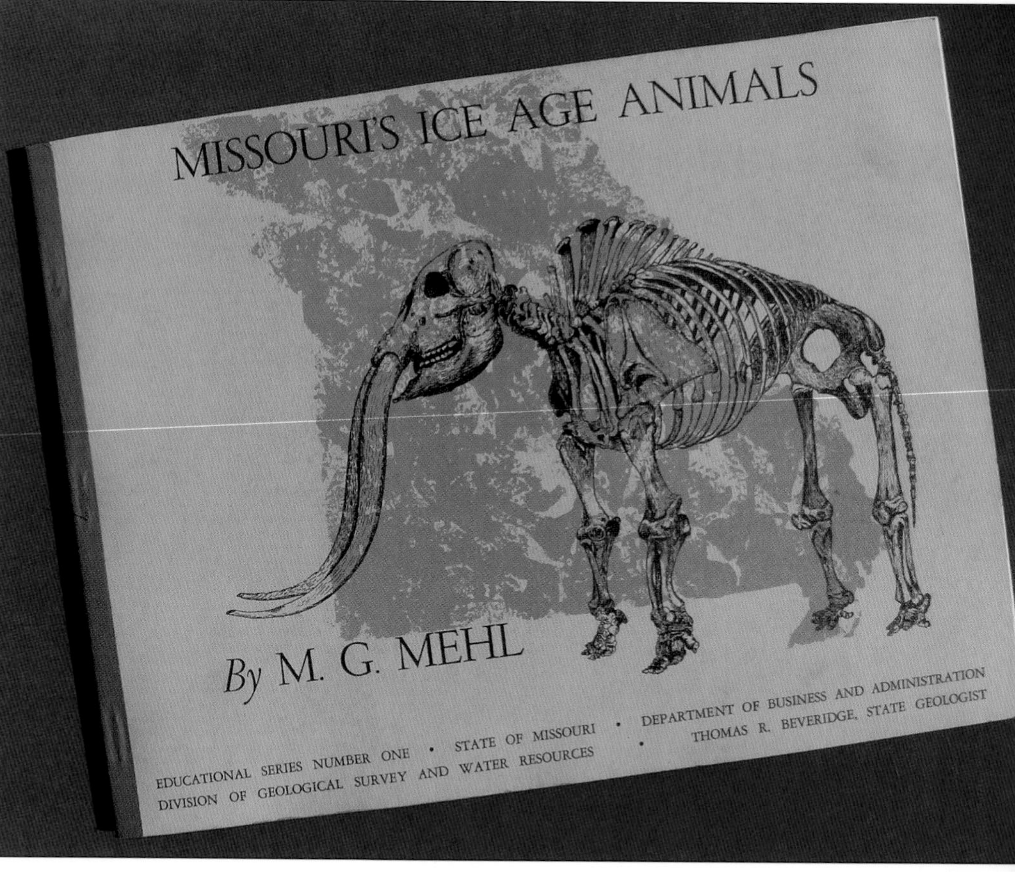

Figure 06-008. Probably the best known and most widely distributed work by Maurice Mehl is his *Ice Age Animals of Missouri*. Mehl verified that the bones found in the Chronister cistern were indeed those of a dinosaur.

Mehl had worked with Mesozoic vertebrate fossils in Wyoming and affirmed that the bones thus found were indeed those of a dinosaur. Steward and Mehl planned to publish a scientific paper on this discovery; however, the fall of 1941 saw the onset of World War II and things drastically changed. Steward focused on strategic mineral deposits of the Joplin area, Willard Farrar was killed in the war (UMR or Missouri University of Science and Technology's Farrar Residence Hall is named after him), and the paper on the Missouri Dinosaur Bones remained in limbo until after the war, when it was published in the *Journal of Paleontology*. Maurice Mehl had contacted Charles Gilmore, a dinosaur expert (worker) with the U S National Museum (Smithsonian Institution) regarding the bones and in 1945 Gilmore coauthored a paper on the site with Steward (Gilmore and Steward, 1945).

Little activity took place at the site until 1972, when the author investigated it and found one of the sons of John and Lula Chronister living nearby. Ole Chronister, the current landowner at the time and one of the sons of John and Lula Chronister, expressed considerable regard for my interest in the site. Attracted to it because of my interest and curiosity about Ozark outliers and their peculiar fossils, it was decided that a backhoe could probe the area around the now abandoned cistern and search for additional bones. Obtaining a small grant from the St. Louis Academy of Science, the site was probed, at first producing nothing but blackish-grey clay. Later digging, however, found bones of both dinosaurs and turtles in grey and yellow clay. A few years after our initial investigations, Ole Chronister offered to sell the site to a person interested in it at a reasonable price and, seeing how other fossil sites are often made unavailable or lost through ownership changes, it was purchased for paleontology. Aware that a site like this has considerable "hands on" educational as well as scientific value, a number of interested persons became involved, including Guy Darrough and Mike Fix of St. Louis. Finding that the site was difficult to work as a consequence of drainage problems and slumping of the clay when wet, the solution to a more or less permanent dig was found in covering the dig site with a plastic tarp-like greenhouse. This is what is currently being utilized to cover the dig to enable the considerable efforts required to expose the bone bearing clay.

Figure 06-009. Dan Steward (left), the geologist who found the dino bones at the Chronister site in a picture taken in 1981. Steward was given bones found in the digging of a cistern on the farm of John and Lula Chronister in 1940. The bones turned out to be those of a dinosaur, the first record of dinosaurs from this part of the United States. Steward later became a geologist with the Eagle Pitcher Company, which operated extensive zinc mines in southwestern Missouri.

Figure 06-010. Group of students from Florissant Valley Community College at the site in 1985. Author is to left of middle with brown sweater. Mike Fix to the left of that.

Figure 06-011. Bill Jud, Dan Steward (left of barrel), and Guy Darrough (blue shirt) at the Chronister Site, 1981.

Figure 06-012. Initial excavation in the area of the cistern, 1978.

Figure 06-013. Backhoe digging at the site where the original dinosaur bones were found in the process of digging a cistern by the Chronisters.

Figure 06-014. A group from southern Methodist University of the Dallas-Fort Worth area looking for possible Mesozoic **mammal** fossils. Most Mesozoic mammals were very small and the clay being dug out here was processed and later searched using a microscope. A backhoe was used to dig into fissures between limestone boulders to obtain clay which might contain early mammal remains in 1979; no fossil mammal remains were found!

Figure 06-015. Same group as in Figure 06-014—a great place for a geology field trip!

Figure 06-016. Working on clay chunks containing dinosaur bones, 1979.

Fossils Found at the Site

The original fossils found in the digging of the cistern in 1940 consisted of fourteen caudal (tail) vertebra of a dinosaur. These tailbones were the bones discussed (figured) in the Gilmore and Steward paper and they formed the basis for establishment of what was considered to be a new (to science) dinosaur to which they gave the name of *Neosaurus missourensis*. The genus *Neosaurus* was coined in view of their belief that the bones belonged to a sauropod, and as such would have been one of the youngest sauropods known (neo=young). When excavations in the mid-1970s produced additional material, assistance in dinosaur taxonomy and anatomy was acquired from David Parris of the New Jersey State Museum. It was found from Parris's examination of the bones that most of the material recovered belonged to hadrosaurs (duckbilled dinosaurs), specifically a hadrosaur of the genus *Hypsibema*. sp. and **not** to a sauropod. *Neosaurus*, the genus established by Gilmore and Stewart, has now been placed in synonymy under the genera *Parrosaurus* sp. and *Hypselbema* sp. Other dinosaur material found consisted of carnosaur bone and teeth (*Albertasaurus* sp.) and gastroliths.

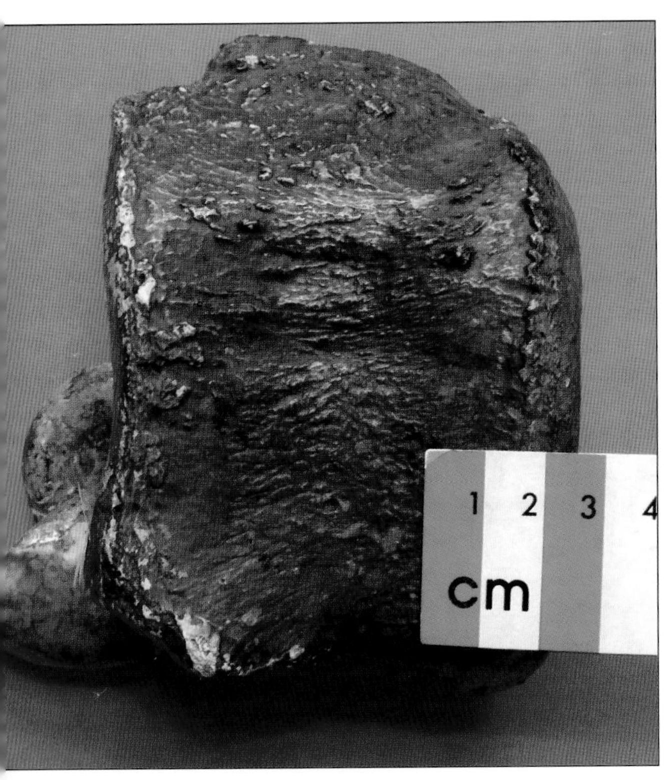

Figure 06-017. Dinosaur vertebra exhibiting evidence of osteoarthritis from the Chronister site.

Figure 06-019. Stuck vehicle at the Chronister site loaded with clay chunks from the site. The clay masses were later "dissolved" and processed for the bones of small Cretaceous mammals which they might contain. None were found, nor have any been found since, although the site still has potential for these elusive fossils – its just finding a zone where they might occur.

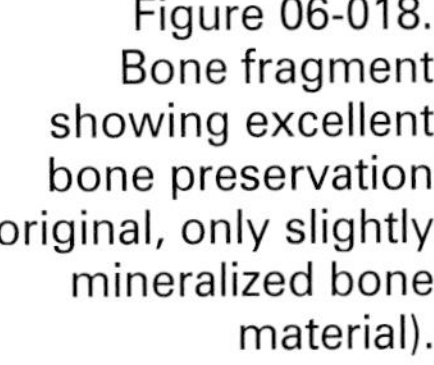

Figure 06-018. Bone fragment showing excellent bone preservation (original, only slightly mineralized bone material).

Figure 06-020. Trench being cut by a backhoe into homogenous, blue grey clay at the Chronister site. Trenches were cut into the clay beds to find the bone-bearing zones – some of the clay layers totally lack fossils.

Figure 06-021. Yellow (oxidized) and grey (unoxidized) clay at the Chronister Site, both types have been found to contain fossil bones and turtle shell fragments.

Figure 06-022. Dozer cutting into clay bed, 1985.

Figure 06-023. Pointing to large, highly weathered bones in yellow clay. When present, bones are often hard to see in the clay, particularly if they are in the oxidized and weathered (yellow) clay, where they are also very fragile.

Figure 06-024. Mike Fix prospecting in the area of a backhoe trench. In the clay were found one of many large, weathered bones, but most of these could not be salvaged.

Figure 06-025. Plaster jacket applied to one of the large weathered bones to enable its extraction from the clay. Fossil bones can be crumbly; covering such a friable bone with a plaster jacket will allow for its extraction; later it can be strengthened by resins and prepared. 1979.

Figure 06-026. Close-up of plaster jacket on a large bone.

Figure 06-027. The large bone (pelvis?) removed from the plaster jacket and prepared.

Figure 06-028. Crocodile scutes and turtle bones are found, sometimes in considerable numbers, particularly after the clay weathers or is sieved for small fossils; here the author is looking for them!

Figure 06-029. Group of students from Florissant Valley Community College looking for small fossils in weathered clay.

Figure 06-030. Excavation of the area east of the cistern where the original dinosaur tail bones (caudal vertebra) were found in 1940. This is the location of the greenhouse currently covering the site.

Figure 06-031. Students from St. Louis Community College, in the Florissant Valley, on a geology field trip, which included the Chronister site.

Figure 06-032. One of numerous smashed turtles of the genus *Adocus*. At some spots in the clay, smashed turtle specimens like this are found stacked one on top of another like so many (broken) pancakes. They may have been smashed and fragmented by dinosaurs walking on the shells of dead turtles ("dinoturbation") or they may have been buried intact and later fragmented by extensive movement of the masses of clay. Such movement may have come from seismic activity (earthquakes) accompanying movement associated with the opening of what could be a small rift zone. (Value range F for similar material).

Turtle remains were also recovered, usually in a very fragmentary condition. Most of this turtle material is from the genus *Adocus* sp., a common late Mesozoic turtle that is related to the still-living, fresh water turtle *Trionyx*. A peculiar beaded turtle of the genus *Naomichelys* was also found, this being a type of turtle more common to the Jurassic than to the Cretaceous. In a portion of the site not covered by the greenhouse but near it was found a large number of specimens of *Adocus* sp. where a novel mechanism explaining their high concentration was suggested by Forir, M. and Stinchcomb, 1996.

Figure 06-033. Another smashed shell from the "turtle stack."

Figure 06-034. Yet another (really smashed) smashed turtle shell.

Figure 06-035. Clay chunk full of turtle fragments, all of the fragments probably came from the same animal.

Figure 06-036. Turtle shell fragments from the Chronister site. Such fragments can be common in non-marine Cretaceous rocks like that of Hell Creek, Montana, or the Lance Creek area of Wyoming. Such material is more unique however when coming from an exotic locality like the Missouri Dino site. (Value range G for box of fragments).

Figure 06-037. Another group of turtle fragments from the Chronister Site.

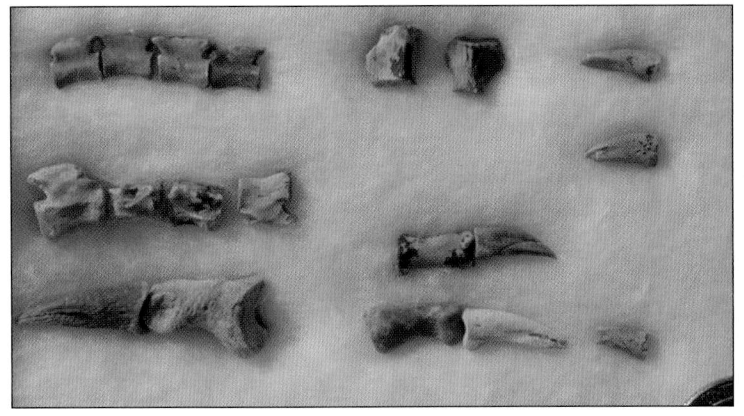

Figure 06-038. "Turtle toes:" Small bones associated with crushed turtle specimens. (Value range G, for group).

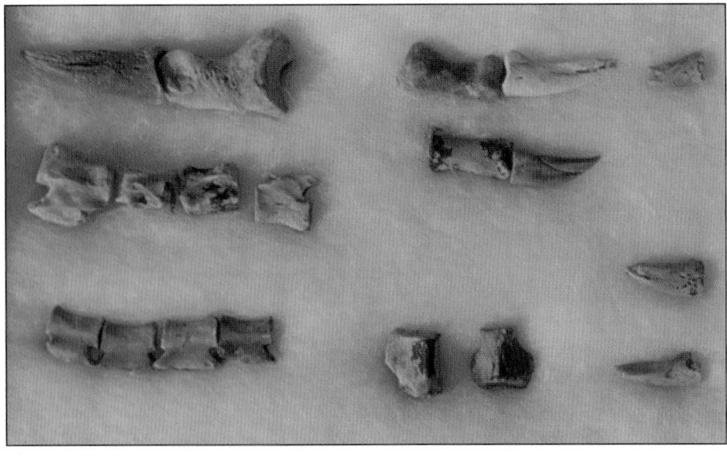

Figure 06-039. Another group of turtle "toes" and claws. *Adocus* sp.

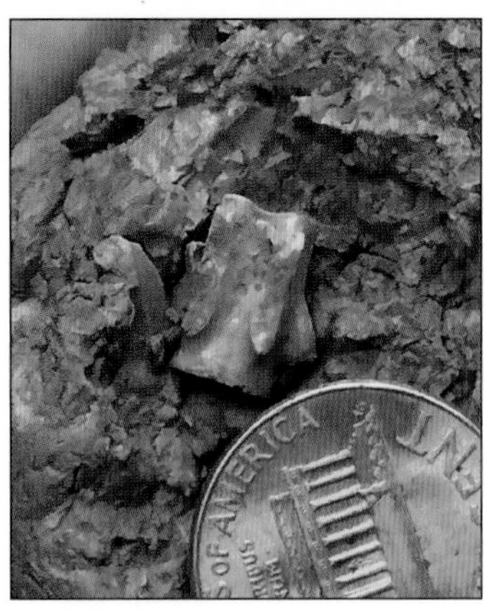

Figure 06-040. Vertebra of *Adocus* in grey clay, Chronister site.

Figure 06-041. Portions (fragments) of the peculiar beaded turtle *Namocheyles* sp. Fragments of this turtle are found in clay pockets over a significant portion of the site. Large complete pieces of this turtle are rare. (Value range E).

Figure 06-042. Large portion of a *Namocheyles* plastron.

Figure 06-043. Close-up of bottom of the plastron of *Namocheyles* showing "beads" on the plastrons surface.

Figure 06-044. Ventral (top) portion of the right part of a *Namocheyles* plastron.

Figure 06-045. Weathered and fragmented *Namocheyles* compared with a relatively unweathered specimen.

Figure 06-046. A pinnacle of dolomite located at the edge of a large sinkhole (Slaughter Sink) in the central Ozarks. Similar steep pinnacles or ledges like this may have surrounded the watering hole which is now the Chronister site. One suggestion explaining the smashed turtles is that turtles climbed onto these high ledges to sun themselves only to fall onto the boulders, which also periodically fell from the cliffs.

The site is considered to have originally been a watering hole as many of the dinosaur bones exhibit bite marks of two types: one associated with scavenging, the other associated with predation (Forir, M., 2001). The sites location appears to be in association with a major fault and bone bearing sediments were probably preserved by downfaulting in a graben (Fix, M., 2001).

Figure 06-047. Crocodile scutes. Chronister site. Crocodile scutes like this can be common fossils in non-marine Cretaceous rocks. These scutes, from the Chronister site, are more desirable when they come from an exotic locality. (Value range G for similar material).

Figure 06-048. Various dinosaur bones, including a collarbone.

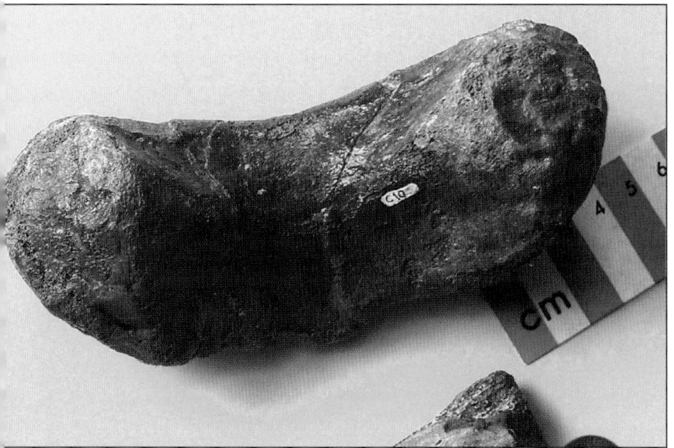

Figure 06-049. Close-up of dino collarbone

Figure 06-050. Another view of a Chronister Site collarbone.

Figure 06-051. Many of the bones at the site show bite marks, which were produced when the bone was still "green," indicating that it may have been gnawed on by scavengers. Bite marks on many of the bones, and the broken nature of the bones, suggests that the site may have been a watering hole for animals.

Local Geologic Structure and Sediments of the Chronister Site

Cretaceous sediments of the Chronister site have been considered to have been preserved by the following phenomena:

A. A filled sinkhole or paleokarst developed in carbonate rocks of the Roubidoux and Jefferson City formations. Filled sinks or sinkholes appear to explain many of the occurrences of isolated, younger age rocks (outliers) found scattered over the Ozarks. The sinkhole filled with an amount of sediment which was greater than that present in the surrounding area during some part of geologic time. This greater thickness of sediment acted as a cap or armor plate, which, when extensive erosion took place, defied removal while the surrounding area was worn down. Such an armor "cap" resulted in what once was a low area (sinkhole), now being (sometimes) the top of an Ozark "Mountain" or knob.
B. A sediment filled graben associated with extensive southeastern Missouri faulting was preserved from erosion in a down-dropped fault block. The fault, being one of many in the Marble Hill-Glen Allen area, an area of complex, "jumbled" geology, was apparently particularly active during the late Cretaceous.
C. A combination of both A and B, that is a fault block along which there was considerable solution of surrounding carbonate rocks producing large sink holes accompanied by the filling of the graben by Late Cretaceous (Campanian) fossil-rich sediments.

One of many puzzles of the Chronister site is the presence of large boulders of "exotic" rocks embedded in the bone bearing clay. These rocks consist primarily of sandstone boulders and boulders of a white limestone (Plattin Limestone) as well as other "exotic" boulders (Bainbridge and Bailey formations). Rock surrounding and outside of the Chronister site valley consists of much older strata of Lower Ordovician age. One novel suggestion explaining these exotic boulders proposes that a cliff face of the younger rocks, now found as boulders in the clay, once surrounded the site which, during the Late Cretaceous, was a deep depression. Boulders of younger rock making up the cliff face would fall into this depression and become buried in fine-grained clay along with the bones of animals attracted to what was a watering hole (Forir and Stinchcomb, 1996).

Figure 06-052. Gnaw marks on another part of a long bone, which is probably from a dinosaur or crocodile.

Figure 06-055. A group of presumed dinosaur (but possibly crocodile) vertebra from the Chronister site.

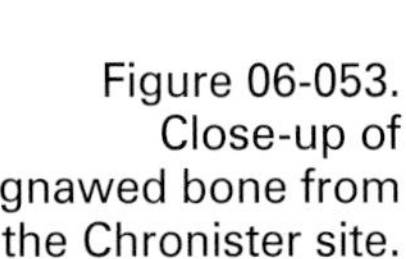

Figure 06-053. Close-up of gnawed bone from the Chronister site.

Figure 06-056. Vertebra from *Hypselbema missourensis*.

Figure 06-054. Gastroliths. These highly polished pebbles are found associated with the dinosaur bones. They are believed to be rocks that were swallowed either by dinosaurs or crocodiles to aid in the grinding of their food. Some of them may also have been polished by fine sediments carried by streams draining into the watering hole.

Figure 06-057. Single vertebra of *H. missourensis* (Gilmore and Steward 1945).

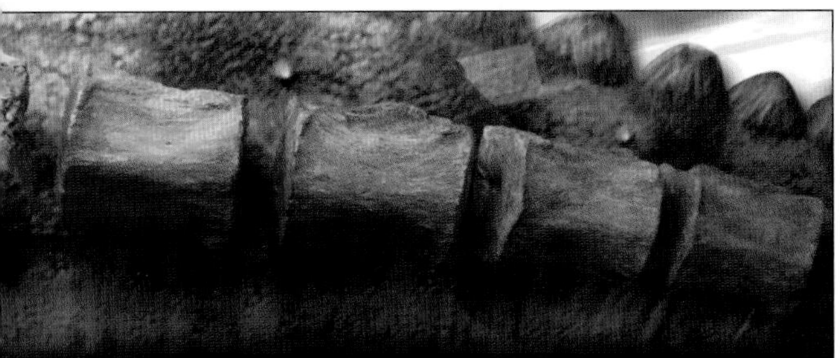

Figure 06-058. Cast of part of the original vertebra found in the Chronister cistern in 1941. These were described by Gilmore and Steward in 1945, as vertebra of a sauropod. Later the bones were recognized by Dave Parris of the New Jersey Museum of Natural History as representative of a hadrosaur or duck billed dinosaur. Specimens on display at the Bollinger County Museum of Natural History.

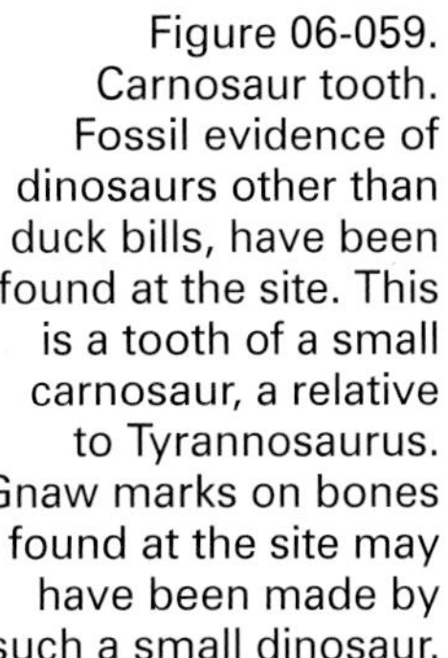

Figure 06-059. Carnosaur tooth. Fossil evidence of dinosaurs other than duck bills, have been found at the site. This is a tooth of a small carnosaur, a relative to Tyrannosaurus. Gnaw marks on bones found at the site may have been made by such a small dinosaur.

Figure 06-060. Metal model of a small carnosaur of the size and type which bore teeth like those of the above specimen.

Figure 06-061. Enlarged photo of bite marks found on many bones at the Chronister site and probably made by a small carnosaur like that in Figure 06-060.

Figure 06-064. Casts of a group of toe bones found at the Chronister site from a large hadrosaur, probably *Hypselbema missourensis*.

Figure 06-062. Ossified tendons. These bony or mineralized tendons are characteristic of hadrosaurs and can occur with some abundance, usually with other hadrosaur remains. They probably are from *Hypselbema missourensis*, the Missouri Dinosaur. (Value range G, similar material).

Figure 06-065. Arrangment of original toe bones into part of a large dinosaur foot. These specimens are now in the Bollinger County Natural History Museum, Marble Hill, Missouri.

Figure 06-063. More ossified tendons of hadrosaurs.

Figure 06-066. Group of skull fragments from a hadrosaur dinosaur, probably *Hypselbema missourensis*.

Figure 06-067. A tooth battery and partial skull of a hadrosaurine dinosaur, probably *Hypselbema missourensis*.

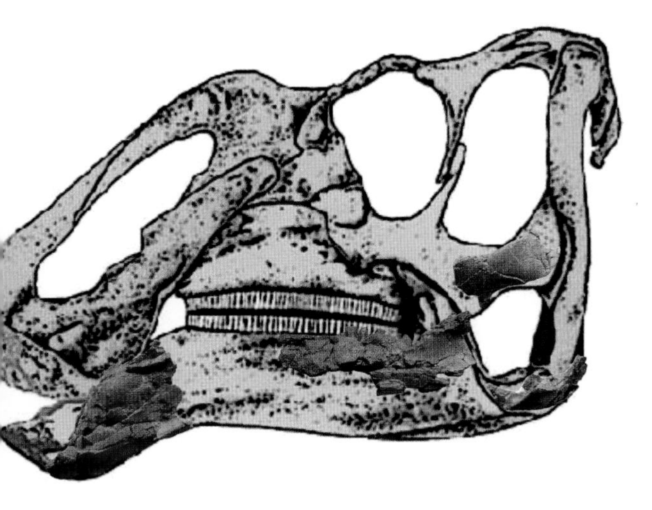

Figure 06-068. The skull fragments of previous photo shown superimposed on a schematic of a hadrosaur skull. *Courtesy of Mike Fix, Univ. of Missouri at St. Louis*.

Figure 06-069. Group of vertebra and scapula (left) in a large chunk of bone bearing clay exhibited in the Bollinger County Museum of Natural History.

Investigation of the site is an ongoing activity. With additional excavation and fossil recovery from other clay occurrences (lenses) at the site, additional (and possibly different) material might be obtained. Other outliers of clay in Bollinger and Butler counties, some of which are shown on the 1979 state geological map (but not on the current one) may also yield additional fossil vertebrate and plant material, possibly some of different age than the Campanian age strata of the Chronister site.

Figure 06-070. Another clay mass with numerous dinosaur bones on exhibit at the Bollinger County Museum of Natural History, Marble Hill, Missouri.

Figure 06-071. Another view of one of the large bone bearing clay chunks.

"Kamikaze" Turtles

Anomalous (puzzling) geology is a characteristic of the Chronister Site. As discussed above, boulders of limestone and sandstone, rocks alien to the immediate surrounding region, are found embedded in the clay along with the bones of dinosaurs and broken up turtle shells. How these "out of place" rocks got there is still one of the mysteries of the site. The best explanation to date remains that

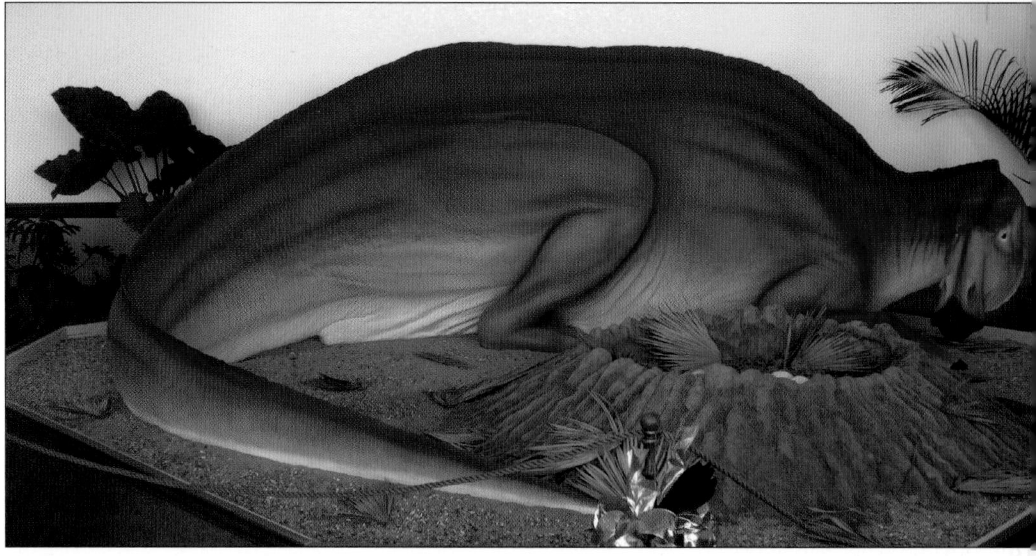

during the Cretaceous Period, there was a sinkhole at the site, which had much higher walls than currently exist. These exotic rocks, within those walls, upon falling into the sink hole, were buried in clay along with the dinosaurs bones and preserved in the fine grained, impervious clay while limestone walls of the sinkhole were dissolved away over millions of years—dissolved by the tropical climate which existed through much of the Cenozoic Era. An accompanying anomalous feature found in the clay are large numbers of smashed fossil turtles, sometimes almost piled one on top of the other.

Figure 06-072. Life-sized fiberglass model of *Hypselbema missourensis* (The Missouri Dinosaur) made by Guy Darrough. This model is now on display at the Bollinger County Museum of Natural History, Marble Hill, Missouri.

Mat Forir, one of my former students, noted and showed me on a canoe trip, how the shells of unfortunate (but stupid) tortoises can be concentrated among the talus or scree at the base of Ozark river bluffs. Tortoises, when walking through the woods, when they come to the edge of a high bluff just keep going, they then fall down the cliff onto the rocks below, usually with fatal results. This behavior can result in an accumulation of considerable numbers of tortoise shells over hundreds of years, the shells of which are usually preserved in the limy environment of the talus. A similar scenario is suggested by Matt for the large, soft shelled turtles at the Chronister site. During the Mesozoic, when the wall of the sink hole was considerably higher than it is today, turtles would climb out of the wet sink hole and find their way onto the surrounding bluff, perhaps to sun themselves in the warm Cretaceous sun. Like the not-too-smart tortoises of eighty million years later, these turtles, when being startled by dinosaurs at the bottom of the sinkhole, would quickly move but would then fall 100+ feet into the sinkhole where they often would hit on a rock or perhaps stunned -- would sink into the mud with accompanying fatal results. Such a scenario, playing out over many years, accumulated quantities of turtle shells which today can be found almost stacked like a pile of pancakes, be they broken ones.

Bibliography

Farrar, Willard and Lyle McManamy, 1937. *The Geology of Stoddard County, Missouri.* Appendix VI, 59th Biennial Report, Missouri Geological Survey and Water Resources.

Fix, Michael F.. 2001. (abstract) "Dinosauria and Associated Vertebrate fauna of the late Cretaceous Chronister site of Missouri." Abstract of 7th North American Paleontological Convention, Univ. of California, Berkley.

Forir, Matthew and Bruce Stinchcomb, 1996. "Peculiar Occurrence of the Cretaceous Turtle *Adocus* at the Chronister site, Bollinger County, Missouri." Sixth North American Paleontological Convention Abstracts of Papers. The Paleontological Society Special Publication No. 8, p. 126. 2001.

Forir, Matthew. (abstract) "Using Taphonomy to determine Paleontological Parameters of the Chronister Local Fauna, Bollinger County, Missouri." Abstracts of 7th North American Paleontological Convention-2001, Univ. of California, Berkley.

Gilmore, Charles W. and Dan Steward, 1945. "A new Sauropod Dinosaur from the Upper Cretaceous of Missouri." *Journal of Paleontology*, Vol. 19 pg 23-29.

Heller, Robert, 1943. *Geology of the Marble Hill Area, Bollinger County, Missouri*: Unpublished Master of Arts Thesis, Graduate School of the University of Missouri, Columbia, 109 pg. map.

Parris, David C., Barbara Grandstaff, and Bruce Stinchcomb, 1988. (abstract) "Chronister, The Missouri Dinosaur Site." (abstract) *Journal of Vertebrate Paleontology* Vol. 8, Supplement to No. 3., Society of Vertebrate Paleontology, Tyrrell Museum of Paleontology. Drumheller, Alberta.

Stinchcomb, Bruce L.,2005. (abstract) "Knob forming distinctive Chert-breccia boulders of the central Ozarks" *in* Evans, Horton Jr., Thompson, and Warme, *The Sedimentary Record of Meteorite Impacts*. SEPM Research Conference, Springfield, Missouri.

Cope and Marsh

Edwin Drinker Cope and Charles Orthaniel Marsh were originally friends near the close of the Civil War. The "antics" of these two vertebrate paleontologists have been outlined before but for comparative purposes will be summarized here. After the Civil War, territory west of the Mississippi River really began to be investigated. Investigated not only for agricultural and settlement purposes but also for its potential paleontological riches, all of which was aided considerably by the construction of the railroads. The last third of the nineteenth century would witness paleontological discoveries on an almost unprecedented scale accompanied by parallel discoveries of mineral wealth. Whole new fossil floras, new invertebrate and vertebrate fossil faunas were discovered and these were documented in a plethora of scientific papers, a major part of which focused on the Mesozoic Era. Such paleontological riches were documented in publications of various state, provincial, and federal geological surveys as well as by various state and provincial academies of science, and after 1880 also by publications of the Geological Society of America. Of this material, most of which was new to science, it was the discovery of Mesozoic ruling reptiles that held the greatest fascination for the public and foremost among the discovers of these big reptile fossils was Edwin D. Cope and Charles O. Marsh. When fossil bones of many of the large vertebrates began to really come onto the scene in western discoveries, Cope and Marsh became at first competitive protagonists and then, as a consequence of a series of incidents, bitter enemies who vied to be the first to discover and document new paleontological finds which were turning up at an alarming frequency.

Marsh was affiliated with the U. S. National Museum (Smithsonian Institution) and had the benefit of an interest in languages and, having become conversant in native American languages such as Arapaho, Navajo and Lakota Sioux, took advantage of this skill in directly communicating with Native Americans. This communications advantage, particularly with tribal chiefs, in their own tongue, enabled Marsh to be privy to areas which tribal leaders knew contained concentrations of large bones, such bones being considered sacred to many Indians. Cope, with backing from the American Museum of Natural History as well as from other institutions, resented Marsh's being privy to this information and both parties periodically hired scouts to spy on each other and find out what was going on in each others' camps.

Figure 06-073. Bollinger County Museum of Natural History, 207 Mayfield Drive, Marble Hill, Missouri 63764.

Figure 06-074. Building-side painting in Marble Hill (The Dinosaur capital of Missouri) of two hadrosaurs accompanied by ever-present erupting volcanoes.

Figure 06-075. Voracious Tyrannosaur on building-side mural, Marble Hill, Missouri.

At times, hostilities became so intense that Indians and U S Army personal engaged in some minor skirmishes predicated upon the dinosaur bones coveted by both parties, the "bone wars" of vertebrate paleontology. Cope also tried, apparently successfully, to woo groups of Indians over to his side, using various strategies, which included his periodically removing and inserting his false teeth, a stunt that totally fascinated the Indian observers. Cope's eagerness, intense desire, and interest in fossil bones also assisted his efforts with the Indians leaving him alone. Indians were sometimes a problem with geological exploration groups like that of Cope and Marsh, however, they refrained from molesting Cope as they believed that the spirits would frown on interference with a **crazy man**.

Marsh, with his focus on Native American ethnology and his Smithsonian connection was instrumental in helping found a Federal Department of Ethnology in the late 1880s. The mission of this federal agency was an attempt to document and preserve various aspects of the culture, languages, and dialects of the American Indian, which were then being severely affected and infringed upon by both settlers and technology. One of the methods he used to accomplish this endeavor was to record these languages and their dialects on the cylinder phonograph of Thomas Edison.

Both Cope and Marsh remained bitter enemies to their last days, which to both of them came at the close of the nineteenth century. Is there something about dinosaur bones that makes bitter enemies of those who laboriously engage in their extraction? Many Indians considered such large bones sacred and that their molestation would incur the wrath of bad spirits, a scenario that seems to have been reenacted in its own way at the Chronister Site.

Figure 06-076. Skinny, elongate dinosaurs (*Camptosaurs*?) with pterdactyals on building side mural, Marble Hill, Mo.

Figure 06-078. Billboard on I-55 north of Cape Girardeau, Missouri, with Missouri Dinosaur.

Figure 06-077. Peculiar, erupting volcano, a variation on the proverbial Mesozoic-erupting-volcano graces this building-side illustration. Is the Triceratops engulfed in lava? Volcanic activity was actually quite widespread in the Late Cretaceous at the time that Triceratops lived. Volcanic ash (bentonite) has also been provisionally identified at the Chronister Site. (It might be noted that no ceratopsian dinosaurs have been found in Cretaceous rocks of the eastern part of North America.) Ceratopsians, particularly Triceratops, appear to have been confined to that part of the continent west of the seaway, which split the continent. (The North American Mediterranean).

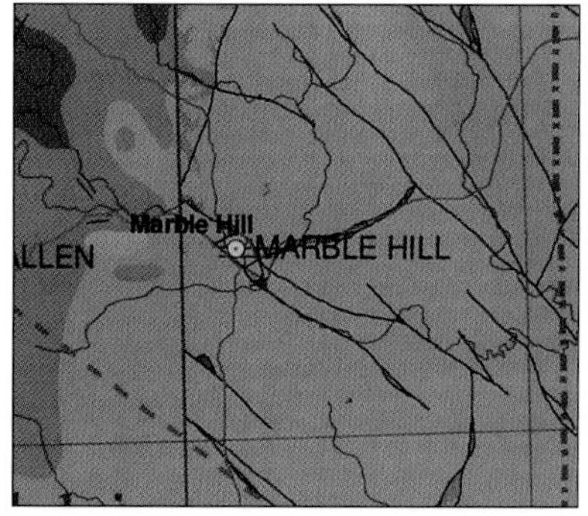

Figure 06-079. A portion of the 2003 Missouri geologic map showing the area around Marble Hill, Missouri. Geologic complexity shown on the 1979 geologic map of the same area is now absent. Cretaceous outliers, including the one forming the Chronister site, are also absent. Other outliers shown on the '79 map are also missing in this version of the Geological map of Missouri. It should be mentioned that geologic maps often include a subjective interpretative element and this may vary with the mapmaker's interpretation of geology, which can even include politics. Absence of the 1979 geologic features on the 2003 map possibly involves such.

A Modern Day "Cope and Marsh" Debacle

Two industrious workers, we shall call them parties A and B, are involved here. After the author's decision to focus more intensely on the Mesozoic fossils of the Chronister Site, he set up to prospect for dinosaur bones using techniques similar to that involved in uranium exploration. If the prospect looked good, it was proposed to dig east of the original cistern site, but this was thwarted by severe water problems. After seeing each dig attempt fill with water after the first rain and collapse, plans were made to cover the site with a plastic greenhouse. Such a cover would prevent water from entering and flooding the site, plus it would also protect the bone bearing clay from the weather. What was not anticipated were the suspicions of local law enforcement authorities who were wary of a greenhouse, which air surveillance had detected, sprouting up in the middle of Ozark woods, and which seemed a sure indication of the growth or formulation of some "controlled substance," substances of which the Ozarks have become infamous for and whose production represents a modern replay of rotgut whiskey production, which the Ozarks were also infamous for during the 1920s Prohibition years.

The two parties, A and B, after meeting each other a few times, quickly acquired an animosity toward each other, seemingly of a magnitude equal to that between Cope and Marsh. After assuring both protagonists that party B would not dig within ten feet of the greenhouse, a line was drawn separating the two areas. Such a line was determined by two points, one, an oak tree, the other, a yucca plant; it was agreed that neither party would go past this imaginary line in either their prospecting or digging activities. A few months passed and when party B arrived to commence prospecting in his allotted territory, the defining yucca had moved by some eight feet, now growing at its new location where the yucca-oak tree line prevented digging at a predetermined location suspected of being rich in fossils. Not to be thwarted by such a "moving line", party B dug anyway, advancing toward the greenhouse where at the end of the dig the yucca mystically transported "itself" to a new position that was now only five feet from the greenhouse. When party A, a few days later, dug inside the greenhouse, the yucca plant again moved to prevent the dig of party B. Such an animated, mysterious jumping yucca plant dominated the dig until both parties tired of these antics and both found a number of time consuming fossil turtles which, in their assembly, detracted both from dinosaurs and yucca plants but the animosity remains to this day. Is this a vestige of the "bad spirits" routed by disturbance of the sacred dinosaur bones of former Indian inhabitants?

Figure 06-080. Artist interpretation of the Chronister site in the late Cretaceous some eighty million years ago (Campanian). The dinosaur in the foreground is *Hypselbema missourensis*. The bluff in the background forms the edge of a sinkhole-graben, which hosts the watering hole. Note concentration of turtles (*Adocus*) sunning themselves on the bluff's edge. The crocodile was one of the large predators and scavengers at the site. This interpretation uses the geologic model of a down dropped fault block or graben for the site. The bluff in the background would have been composed of younger rocks which today make up the exotic boulders now found embedded in the bone bearing clay. All traces of this bluff are now gone, presumably having been removed by weathering and erosion. *Artwork by William Brownfield*.

Figure 06-081. Late Cretaceous Pterodactyls. Igneous rock (nepheline syenite) was intruded into strata of the Gulf Embayment during the late Cretaceous to form what would become the Fourche Mountains south of Little Rock, Arkansas—similar igneous activity occurred elsewhere along the Gulf Embayment, which formed a northward extension of the Gulf of Mexico during the late Cretaceous and the early Cenozoic. Surface extensions of these peculiar igneous rocks are shown here serving as perches for flying reptiles, which flew out over the shallow Cretaceous seaways of Arkansas and southeastern Missouri. *Artwork by Elizabeth V. Stinchcomb.*

Glossary

Archeological Model (applied to paleontology): A site or locality management model and philosophy applied to archeological sites. Such sites are generally limited and their archeological resources confined to a small area. As a consequence of this relatively limited resource (artifacts), collecting by individuals is usually discouraged. This model is, however, usually inappropriate to paleontology as fossils occur in strata and such strata generally cover or underlie relatively large areas—access to its fossils being limited to the existence of outcrops of a particular fossil bearing layer rather than being limited by the actual amount of the resource present as is often the case with archeology.

Bentonite: A type of clay derived from the alteration of volcanic ash. Bentonite is particularly characteristic of the late Cretaceous worldwide where beds of it can be of considerable thickness where they are sometimes mined. Bentonite, upon getting wet, swells and becomes impervious; because of this property it is frequently used to seal leaks in building foundations and dams. Soils containing bentonite, on becoming wet, also become incredibly slippery and also swell, moving and disturbing whatever is upon them, including buildings and roads.

Chalcedony: A very finely crystalline (Cryptocrystalline) form of quartz that can appear milky or grey and homogeneous in appearance. In reference to quartz replaced dinosaur eggs from Argentina and is referred to in Chapter Five.

Coccoliths and Rhabdoliths: Very small (10-30 microns) calcareous spicules from extinct, photosynthetic protists which lived in abundance in the seas of the late Mesozoic. They represent a biochemical sediment and are a major component of chalk.

Concretions: Globular or potato-shaped masses of harder composition than the enclosing rock. Being harder than the enclosing sedimentary rock, concretions can weather out and accumulate on hillsides or in streams. Concretions sometimes enclose well-preserved fossils, as is the case with the fish bearing Lower Cretaceous examples of the Santana Formation of Brazil. Concretions (and related phenomena like nodules) are also sometimes mistaken for dinosaur eggs by the uninformed.

Geode: A hollow, crystal-lined spherical rock which is often collectable for its crystallized mineral specimens. In Chapter Five geodes are mentioned in reference to dinosaur eggs from Argentina, which can be filled with quartz crystals like those found in a geode.

Graben: A part of a planetary surface produced from the existence of **tension** on a planetary surface. A graben is composed of two faults more or less parallel to each other with material between the two faults moving down by gravity (downdropped). One of the best examples of a graben can be seen on the planet Mars where the Valles Marineris forms a conspicuous feature on the planets surface. Another large (and obvious) graben on the Earth's surface is the region of the Red Sea. Downdrop fault zones are also known as **Rift zones** in Plate Tectonics. In this book, the Missouri Dinosaur Site (Chronister Site) probably occupies a small rift zone or graben.

Gulf Series: A sequence of (often soft and unconsolidated) rock strata surrounding the Gulf of Mexico. Such strata ranges in age from Jurassic to the late Cenozoic (Neogene). Cretaceous rocks can constitute a major part of Gulf Series sediments and can sometimes be rich in fossils.

Heteromorph Ammonites: An ammonite having a shell which is different in shape (Morphology) from that of a "normal" ammonite coil. Heteromorphs take on a variety of shapes, but a distinctive one is a form that turns back on itself and resembles a saxophone. The maximum development of heteromorphs was in the latest Cretaceous, Campanian, and Maastrichtian. Heteromorph ammonites have been explained as a consequence of some sort of taxonomic or "racial" senility as their maximum development in the late Cretaceous was followed by their extinction.

High Grade Metamorphic Rock: Metamorphic rock is rock which has been changed as a consequence of pressure (usually associated with mountain building) or from deep burial within the Earth's crust; the parent rock can either be igneous or sedimentary. Generally metamorphic rock is of considerable geologic age but this is not always the case. With regards to the Cretaceous Period, metamorphic rock of this age is found worldwide and specific areas mentioned are the "basement" rocks of the Caribbean, specifically Jamaica, and in Alaska. High-grade metamorphic rock can also be a source of sediment, which composes younger rock, as is the case with mica derived from mica schist making up track bearing layers on Crowley's Ridge in southeastern Missouri.

Irregular Echinoids: A sea urchin (echinoid) order which appeared and became abundant in the Lower Cretaceous. Prior to the Cretaceous, echinoids generally have a radial (five-sided or pentameral) symmetry as represented by the cidarids, which are the **regular** echinoids. **Irregular** echinoids have a bi-lateral symmetry imposed upon a radial or pentameral symmetry.

Joint: A "crack" in rock of the Earth's crust produced by either earth movement (tectonic forces) or from the release of pressure or weight when overlying rock layers are removed by weathering and erosion.

K/T boundary: A rather sharp boundary in the rock (or stratigraphic) record delineated by an abrupt change in the fossil content of sedimentary rocks deposited sixty-seven million years ago. This boundary separates the Cretaceous (K) from the Tertiary Period (T) of the Cenozoic Era. A "**spike**" delineated by the occurrence of the trace element **iridium** is found at this boundary and this has been attributed to material vaporized from an asteroid(s) which fell sixty-seven million years ago. Many asteroids contain iridium (one of the platinum group elements) as a sub-major component. Iridium is rare in the Earth's crust, as most of it resides in the Earth's core, but it is abundant in asteroids. Mass extinctions occurring at the K/T boundary are attributed to these asteroidal impacts.

Lithophysae: Spherical structures associated with beds of volcanic ash (tuff) in regions of felsic (continental) volcanic activity. Sometimes such structures are hollow and contain crystals as in a **geode**. They are collected and polished by rockhounds and commonly known as **thunder eggs**.

Magma: Molten rock within the Earth. When magma comes to the Earth's surface it becomes lava or is blown out as volcanic ash. During the Late Cretaceous exceptional amounts of magma were extruded from the Earth's mantle to form a rise of the oceans' floors as this magma upwelled at the mid-oceanic ridges. These enlarged **spreading centers** displaced large volumes of sea water, some of which spread over parts of the continents.

MAPS EXPO: A fossil fair or show put on yearly by the **M**id **A**merican **P**aleontological **S**ociety, which has been and is held in the early Spring in McComb, Illinois. MAPS EXPO is one of the largest such fossil shows in the world.

Marl: A soft, chalky clay or mudstone deposited under marine conditions. In the Cretaceous, marls can often grade into chalk and in North America chalky marl is often found in place of pure chalk. Marks can locally be rich in fossils, particularly oysters and some types of clams such as inoceramids.

Mid-oceanic Ridges: A rise in the floor of the middle part of the world's oceans. This rise is caused (in part) by extrusion of mafic magma coming from fissures connecting with the Earth's mantle from which the magma originates. Mid-oceanic ridges form one type of plate boundary in **Plate Tectonics**.

Plate Tectonics: A major part of geology and/or geophysics which explains many of the Earth's geologic features (and geographic ones as well) by recognizing on the globe a series of plates which are in relative motion to each other and which are separated from each other by plate boundaries. It is at plate boundaries that many geologic phenomena such as earthquakes and volcanoes occur.

Radiometric Age Dating: A method for determining relatively precise ages of rocks (and their enclosed fossils) through measurements of radioactive elements and the amounts of decay product produced by the parent radioactive element (usually uranium). Radiometric age dating is generally considered to be the most accurate and reliable of the various methods for determining geologic time. Igneous rock associated with volcanic activity such as volcanic ash (tuff or bentonite) is particularly appropriate for radiometric age dating. Igneous material at the end of the Cretaceous has enabled a precise date of the K/T boundary at 67.3 million years.

"Science fiction like aspect of fossils": A phenomena sometimes "felt" or mentioned by persons while digging into a fossil bed. The direct and tangible contact with something so ancient and yet so clearly and distinctively preserved seems like something out of science fiction rather than the reality that it is.

Solnhofen-like Lagerstatten: A sequence of lagoon deposited limestone of Late Jurassic age near the southern German town of Solnhofen, Bavaria, which has yielded a variety of exceptional, complete fossils. A similar series of slabby limestone (plattenkalk) of Lower Cretaceous age, which also preserves exceptionally fine fossils, occurs in the country of Lebanon east of the Mediterranean.

Spreading Centers: The middle part of the world's oceans where molten rock (magma) up-wells from the Earth's mantle, causing both a rise of the ocean's floor and the creation of new oceanic crust, which produces sea floor spreading. Sea floor spreading can transport ocean floor sediments great distances and pile them up against the continents, adding new crust to the continents. Mid-oceanic ridges and spreading centers were particularly active during the late Cretaceous. This activity raised the ocean's floor in proximity to the mid-oceanic ridges, displacing vast amounts of seawater, which then spilled out onto the continents, allowing for the accumulation of large amounts of marine sediments in these marginal oceans.

Taxa: A unit of classification in organismic biology, such as genus or species or other Linnaean category. Derived from taxonomy, the science (and art) of the classification of living things, which includes fossils.

Tectonism (Tectonic activity): Earth movement which includes earthquakes and which is responsible for geologic forces such as uplift and mountain building. The end of the Cretaceous was a time of particularly widespread and extensive tectonism.

Tertiary Period: The major geologic period of the Cenozoic Era. The Tertiary Period follows the Cretaceous and was the time when much of the life of today's world evolved.

Tracks and Trackways: Trace fossils made by the activity of organisms living in the geologic past. Specifically, in the Cretaceous, these are tracks made by vertebrate animals, which can range from dinosaurs, turtles, and lizards to pterosaurs and birds.

Tuffaceous: A sedimentary rock or sediment containing a high percentage of volcanic ash. In the Cretaceous, tuffaceous sediments are found in many parts of the globe.

Volcanoclastic Sediments: Sediment or sedimentary rock containing volcanic ash or other materials derived from volcanic eruptions as one of its major components. In reference to the Cretaceous where volcanic material can be a common component of rocks to an extent greater than that found in sedimentary rocks of other geologic ages.

More Schiffer Titles

www.schifferbooks.com

;ems & Minerals. Dr. Andreas .andmann. More than 150 photos vith descriptions provide an over- 'iew of minerals from all parts of he world and relate how miner- ıls originate, how they are found, ınd what significance they had in ıncient times. Learn to identify the tones, including quartz, feldspar, beryl, tourmaline, orundum, diamond, garnet, spinel, fluroite, precious ıetals, and more.

;ize: 8 1/2" x 11"	166 color photos	180pp.
SBN: 978-0-7643-3066-7	hard cover	$29.99

;ollecting Fluorescent Minerals. ;tuart Schneider. Over 800 beauti- ul color photographs illustrate how luorescent minerals look under the JV light and in daylight, making this ın invaluable field guide. Minerals nclude Aragonite, Celestine, Feld- par, Microcline, Picropharmacolite,)uartz, Spinel, Smithsonite plus ıany more from the United States, Canada, Mexico, ;reenland, Italy, Sweden, and other places. A compre- ıensive resources section, plus helpful advice on car- ng for, collecting, and displaying minerals make this ıne of the most complete references available.

;ize: 8 1/2" x 11"	846 color photos	192pp.
	Price Guide/Index	
SBN: 0-7643-2091-2	soft cover	$29.95

Paleozoic Fossils. Bruce L. Stinchcomb. The rich fossil record of the Paleozoic Era (545 to 300 million years ago) illustrated with 650 high quality color photos and detailed with a very readable text. The photos show the fossil remains of the earth's early animals and plants. A great book for fossil hunters of all ilks interested in early remnants of life.

Size: 8 1/2" x 11"	659 color photos	160pp.
	Value Guide	
ISBN: 978-0-7643-2917-3	soft cover	$29.95

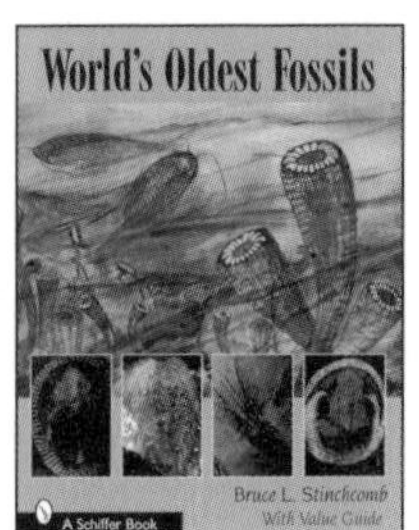

World's Oldest Fossils. Bruce L. Stinchcomb. Covers the earliest fossil record of life from strata called Precambrian and Cambrian by geologists. Illustrated and discussed are structures formed by very primitive photosynthetic life forms, Cambrian trilobites, problematic fossil-like objects, and fascinating paleontological "puzzles." Includes collector information, glossary, value ranges.

Size: 8 1/2" x 11"	509 color photos	160pp.
	Price Guide	
ISBN: 978-0-7643-2697-4	soft cover	$29.95

Schiffer books may be ordered from your local bookstore, or they may be ordered directly from the publisher by writing to:

Schiffer Publishing, Ltd.
4880 Lower Valley Rd.
Atglen, PA 19310
(610) 593-1777; Fax (610) 593-2002
E-mail: Info@schifferbooks.com

Please visit our web site catalog at ***www.schifferbooks.com*** or write for a free catalog. Please include $5.00 for shipping and handling for the first two books and $2.00 for each additional book. Full-price orders over $150 are shipped free in the U.S.

Printed in China

Over 500 photos and engaging text reveal the fossils of the Cretaceous Period, the last period of the Mesozoic Era, the "Age of Reptiles," dating from 120 to 67 million years ago. Included are typical Mesozoic fossils, such as the ammonites, belemnites, and other collectible fossil mollusks characteristic of the Cretaceous, a variety of plants, well-preserved arthropods such as crabs and insects, turtles, crocodiles, and dinosaurs. Fossils recovered range from the Early Cretaceous to the Upper Cretaceous III, ending at the KT boundary representing the events that swept dinosaurs off the face of the planet. Each fossil displayed is carefully identified, along with the region from which it was recovered. The book aids fossil collectors and all who are intrigued about the fascinating artifacts of this early age.

US $29.99

9 780764 332593 52999

ISBN: 978-0-7643-3259-3